Healing Life's Hidden Addictions

Overcoming the Closet Compulsions that Waste Your Time and Control Your Life

Dr. Archibald D. Hart

Servant Publications
Ann Arbor, Michigan

Copyright © 1990 by Archibald D. Hart, Ph.D.
All rights reserved.

Vine Books is an imprint of Servant Publications
especially designed to serve Evangelical Christians.

Published by Servant Publications
P.O. Box 8617
Ann Arbor, Michigan 48107

Cover design by Michael Andaloro
90 91 92 93 94 10 9 8 7 6 5 4 3 2 1
Printed in the United States of America
ISBN 0-89283-668-7

Library of Congress Cataloging-in-Publication Data

Hart, Archibald D.
   Healing life's hidden addictions : overcoming the
closet compulsions that waste your time and control
your life / Archibald D. Hart.
      p.   cm.
   Includes bibliographical references.
   ISBN 0-89283-668-7
   1. Compulsive behavior—Popular works. 2. Co-
dependence (Psychology)—Popular works. I. Title.
RC533.H37 1990
616.85'227—dc20   90-12674
                                                        CIP

To my brother Kenneth

We share so much in common;
we have been through so much together.
My prayers are with you in your healing,
and my appreciation for your caring
grows stronger each passing year.

Contents

ACKNOWLEDGMENTS

As always, the completion of a project like this is never the work of just the author. I am deeply indebted to many for their help:

- to my wife and partner in all my endeavors, Kathleen, for her encouragement, support, and editing help,

- to my secretary, Nova Hutchins, and her patient husband, Paul, for all her typing, advice, and protection from distracting interruptions,

- to Freda Carver and my administrator, Bertha Jacklitch, for their assistance,

- and to Ann Spangler and Beth Feia of Servant Publications, for their invaluable guidance and spiritual encouragement throughout this project.

To all of you I say a deeply felt thank you.

Introduction:
The Addiction Controversy

A CONTROVERSY IS BREWING on the human behavior front. Experts are taking sides and drawing swords.

What about? A simple question: Is *everybody* an addict?

Until recently, you had to "pop a pill" or "shoot up" to be called an addict. And some people still hold that the term *addiction* should be limited to dependence on some external substance. But others claim that human beings can become addicted to *anything*:

> If I long to be on the golf course rather than in a dull meeting, I'm in danger of being labeled a "golfaholic."

> "I love chocolate." You must be *addicted* to chocolate.

> "I enjoy jogging." You must be *addicted* to jogging.

> "I have a passion for gardening." You must be *addicted* to gardening.

> "I love my kids and don't want to see them move away." You must be *addicted* to your kids.

You name it, and we'll call it an addiction!

Who's right? In a way, both sides are!

There is little argument that problems of addiction abound in our society. "Just Say No" is the battle cry of our age. Most people readily accept that alcoholism and drug addiction are a scourge, and most don't hesitate to call these addictions "diseases." They leave a trail of devastating tragedy and indescribable misery behind them. And researchers are uncovering more and more scientific evidence that the term *addiction* does indeed transcend external substances and include many behaviors and emotions.

But this has raised a whole new set of questions. What is addiction all about? How—and to what—does one become addicted? Is addiction a personality defect? Can it be inherited? What causes one person to become addicted to alcohol, another to food, and a third to sex? Is the development of addictions pure chance, or are we each programmed differently? Are all addictions harmful?

And then there is the question of personal choice and moral responsibility. Is addiction a disease, a moral choice, or both? Can addicts help themselves? Are they exempt from personal responsibility?

It's all very confusing, isn't it?

There are no simple answers to these questions—which is why it will take the whole of this book for me to explore the issues. Some experts would unequivocally state that any attachment is an addiction. Psychiatrist Gerald May, for example, who has worked extensively with chemical dependencies, argues quite persuasively that addiction occurs whenever desire is *attached* to some object or behavior. This attachment enslaves our energy to these specific behaviors, things, or people.[1] He believes that the psychological, neurological, and spiritual dynamics of full-fledged addictions are actively at work within *every* human being. The same processes that are responsible for addiction to alcohol and narcotics, he further believes, are responsible for addictions to "ideas, work, relationships, power, moods, fantasies, and an endless variety of other things." He goes so far as to suggest that "we are all addicts in every sense of the word."[2]

At the other end of the opinion spectrum are those who argue, just as persuasively, that the term *addiction* must be reserved for genuine drugs like heroin or cocaine. Most will concede alcohol as well and, when pushed, nicotine and caffeine, which involve clearly observable physical withdrawal symptoms (although these last two are considered "minor" drugs). But these and these only, they insist, are "addictions."

The whole concept of "codependency" is often cited as an example of taking the concept of addiction too far. The term *codependency* refers to a person's *need to be needed* by an addict. To be codependent is to be a dependent person's rescuer—thus the prefix *co*. I will devote a later chapter to *this* topic and will explore whether or not it is truly an addiction.

My own opinion, which I base not only on research but also on my years of experience as a therapist, and on which I will elaborate in the chapters to come, lies between these two extremes. I am convinced that addictions to behaviors, activities, and emotions are real and potent—but not every attachment is an addiction.

Before rushing off and labeling every personal idiosyncrasy as an addiction, I believe we need to review the facts carefully. Psychological and spiritual fads come and go, and right now a lot of addiction labeling has a "faddish" feel.

Addictive behavior is being presented in many quarters of our society as our number-one health problem. Seminars and programs are offered far and wide—at costs ranging from nothing to thousands of dollars—on coping with multiple addictions, codependency, and what are sometimes called "minor" addictions: smoking, coffee, work, sex, exercise, religion, and food. Most of the data presented is anecdotal and of doubtful value in the long term. We need much wisdom to make sure we are not creating more of a problem than what actually exists.

In this book, then, I want to examine the limits of the addiction model carefully and seek to clarify not only its appropriate use but also its most effective treatment. Yes, hidden addictions *are* real. But we must not be so naïve as to think that *all* problems can be reduced to one narrow cause or explanation. Life is simply more complicated than that!

Addiction is a complex interaction of psychological, biochemical, neurological, *and* spiritual factors, and treating addictions involves keeping a delicate balance. On the one hand, I believe, it is vital to confront the element of moral responsibility and mobilize the most effective spiritual resources available to deal with these problems. In order to do these things, however, we also need to glean the soundest and best therapeutic advice available from the medical and psychological disciplines to help those who suffer from "hidden" addictions. In this book I will share what I have learned both from my own practice and from experts in the field about how hidden addictions can be healed.

This book will follow one theme throughout: addictions (whether to chemicals or behavior) are a problem because they remove us from our true feelings. They dull the awareness of, tolerance for, and experience of *true* existence. They mask or "cover" our essential feelings and thus prevent us from being fully human.

In this sense all addictions are alike. We choose behavior that eventually robs us of control; we voluntarily surrender responsibility for our lives. From a Christian point of view, this is sin at its most fundamental level. Not only does it need treatment; it also needs repentance and all the healing that has been made available through Calvary! The only effective healing I know is the healing that takes place at the "core" of our being. Join me as we rediscover the truthfulness of Isaiah's prophecy: that Christ "took our sicknesses, and bore our diseases," so that we could go free (Mt 8:17 LB).

PART I

Understanding
Hidden Addictions

ONE

What Are Hidden Addictions?

R OGER IS TWENTY-SIX YEARS OLD. Since graduating from high school, he has worked at a variety of jobs, trying unsuccessfully to find a "niche" for himself. He has attended the local city college on and off during that time, trying to finish his college education, but he has been unsuccessful at that, too.

Roger's problem is that he cannot concentrate on any task for too long before he gets bored and becomes distracted by a strong urge to seek out some sexual activity.

The urge is overpowering at times. Once it is upon him, he cannot control it or set it aside. In recent months, the compulsion has reached the point that it is interfering with his everyday life. He can't concentrate on his work, even though the work he does is quite menial and doesn't require a lot of concentration. As a result, he has been fired from several jobs.

Roger became desperate, so he sought out therapy. Interestingly, he had no label for his problem when he first came in, nor did he seem to be able to identify the unusual mechanisms at work. As he began to talk about his problem, a clear picture of sexual addiction emerged. Roger had never been aware of this before.

The most recent event that provoked him to seek help occurred when he was on his way to work several weeks ago. He was driving by a high school when he noticed several attractive older female students talking outside the school. He slowed down to "take a look" and became so obsessed with the girls that he drove around the block to see them again—and again, and again. He just couldn't leave the area of the high school, even though the girls had long since vanished into the school building. The experience frightened Roger because he realized how out of control he was.

As Roger talked he continued to reveal other behavior patterns as well. His preoccupation with sex is playing havoc with his life. His relating skills have become stunted to such an extent that female friends avoid him. Even his male friends are becoming afraid of his strange preoccupations. He feels self-contempt, rage, and the pain of his isolation. And the more rejected he feels, the more obsessed he becomes. He has begun to visit prostitutes, porno shops, and X-rated cinemas on a regular basis; he can't stay away from anything that offers the possibility of sexual gratification—but he never feels fulfilled. No amount of masturbation seems to reduce his sexual appetite. Preoccupation with sex is ruining Roger's life.

OUR HIDDEN ADDICTIONS

Roger, like some ten to thirty percent of Americans, suffers from a "hidden" addiction. In Roger's case, the addiction is to sex. Others are "hooked" on work, watching TV, overeating, running, shoplifting, or even religious activities.

But why do I speak of these problems as "hidden"? For that matter, why do I speak of them as "addictions"? What do they have in common with the more widely recognized addictions to drugs or alcohol? There are three ways in which we can speak of addictions like Roger's as "hidden":

- *The addiction is hidden because the victim is not consciously aware (in the beginning, at least) that it exists.* He or she is oblivious to the addiction and yields to it without any thought or decision.

- *The addiction is hidden because society at large does not recognize the problem as an addiction.* The behavior may even be admired in some circumstances (as in workaholism, for instance).

- *The addiction is hidden because we do not yet fully understand the addicting mechanism.* The control exerted by the problem clearly mimics the control of external substances such as drugs or alcohol. However, the addictive process is less obvious than with these external substances.

There is strong evidence that the mechanism of addiction goes far beyond the taking of some mind-altering substance, and this realization has now led us to seeing addiction as falling into two major categories: *substance* addictions and *process* addictions. "Substance" refers to addiction to an external substance such as drugs, alcohol, nicotine, caffeine, and certain foods. "Process" means a series of activities or interactions that "hook" a person or on which a person becomes dependent.

I like the term "process addiction" because it describes quite accurately what goes on in the addictions to behaviors or activities. It allows for a broad and accurate interpretation of how these addictions are formed. Most hidden addictions—such as workaholism, sex addictions, addiction to religion—fall into this category, although, as I will explain, they may involve dependence on an *internal* substance. (Some of the "minor" substance addictions—such as caffeine, nicotine, or certain foods—can also be classed as "hidden" because they are not condemned by society.)

Table 1 lists some the more common hidden addictions. I would add one word of caution, however. Seeing yourself or someone else on this list—even more than once—doesn't necessarily mean that you or the other person is an addict. Not every pleasure-seeking activity or persistent habit is an addiction; neither is every compulsive or obsessive behavior. In pages to come we will examine more closely the characteristics of a true addiction and look at strategies for recognizing and overcoming hidden addictions. First, however, I'd like to define some terms and look at some characteristics all addictions—hidden or not—have in common.

TABLE 1

Some Forms of Hidden Addiction

arguing	rage
collecting	religious activities
competition	resentment
eating	risk taking (daredevil
emotions (like depression)	(behavior)
fishing	self-punishment
gambling	(masochism)
gossip	sex (fantasy, masturbation)
helping needy people	shoplifting
jogging	shopping
lying	solitude
obsessional thinking	temper tantrums
people	thinking (certain styles)
perfectionism	thrill seeking
pornography	TV
reading	work (workaholism)

WHAT IS AN ADDICTION, ANYWAY?

The term *addiction* is far more difficult to define than you might suppose, particularly from a therapeutic viewpoint. (It doesn't even appear in the standard *Diagnostic Manual of Mental Disorders.*[1]) This is one reason it has been applied so broadly—to cover everything from cocaine abuse to collecting discount coupons.

The dictionary definition of *addicted* is a very general one: "applying or devoting oneself habitually."[2] This definition could even include "good" activities, although the term is commonly applied only to negative behaviors. The Latin root is *addicene*, "to give assent, to assign or surrender"—in ancient times it was used to describe someone (usually an enemy) who was captured and kept in bondage or slavery. This is a good description of the modern addict as well—he or she is a "slave" to an attachment. A person can be considered addicted, then, when an "overpowering, repetitive, excessive need exists for some substance, object, feeling, act, milieu, or personal interaction."[3]

We see, then, that while traditional usage applies the term *addiction* only to the habitual use of narcotics or the like, by definition it can also be applied to other behaviors to which we "give assent" on an habitual basis and which have the power to "enslave" us. These are our hidden addictions.

WHAT DO ALL ADDICTIONS HAVE IN COMMON?

Addictions vary widely in terms of underlying motivation, rapidity of onset, degree of physical and emotional damage, degree of social acceptability, and many other factors. There is one unifying theme, however, that ties all addictions together, linking the substance and process addictions, obvious and hidden ones:

1. *Addictions serve the purpose of removing us from our true feelings and providing a form of escape.* This underlying purpose

remains true no matter what underlying mechanism creates the addiction—whether it is biological, psychological, even spiritual, or all three. Addictions serve the function of helping us avoid the real anxieties of life by disengaging from reality. Unfortunately, as Roger's case shows, they also prove destructive in the long run.

Addictive behaviors have some other interesting similarities as well. The most obvious is lack of control:

2. *Addictions totally control the addict, and the control transcends all logic or reason.* This doesn't mean that addicts lack the responsibility—or the ability—to change. It merely means the attachment is very strong and cannot be overcome or resisted by logic or reason alone. This is one reason addictions are extremely difficult to treat and to overcome.

I may be an avid sailor. I may even neglect my family when I go sailing. I may passionately plead for opportunities to raise my sail and manipulate my schedule to get to the boat. But by no stretch of the imagination can my passion be called an "addiction" unless I am unable by logic or reason to transcend or control it. If I can talk myself out of sailing, it's not likely to be an addiction.

My attachment may be a persistent desire. It may be a powerful obsession (we will discuss the relationship between addictions and obsessions in a later chapter). It may even make me sick. But if I can truly reason with it (as opposed to rationalizing it), *I am not an addict.*

3. *Addictions always involve pleasure.* Addictive behavior invariably provides pleasure of some kind—stimulation, excitement, tranquillity, release, or some other enjoyable feeling—that is directly related to the substance or activity. In the later stages of the addiction, the addict may well dislike the adverse consequences of the addiction, but he or she still finds pleasure in the substance or behavior itself. (This is an important distinction, because it helps clarify the difference between addictions and other neurotic disorders.)

Of course, not every pleasurable activity is an addiction! If this were true, the ideal life would have to be awfully dull. Pleasure itself is not the problem, provided it is sought only occasionally and in moderation. But the long-term effect of constant pleasure-seeking can be devastating.

It behooves all of us, therefore, to pay careful attention to our habits and lifestyles—especially the most dangerous of all: the search for excitement and challenge. The pleasure derived from interesting challenges and demanding schedules can be very misleading because it is the very stuff of which damaging stress is made.

This leads us to the next major characteristic of addiction:

4. *In the long haul, addictions are destructive and unhealthy.* Although an addictive substance or behavior continues to give pleasure, it eventually harms or destroys the body, the mind, and the spirit. It also damages relationships, devastates loved ones, and erodes balanced living.

The hard worker, for example, can only be considered an "addict"—a workaholic—if excessive devotion to work breaks up his or her marriage, or at least creates severe conflict, or if it robs his or her family of normal parental involvement. A father who creates a business empire to pass on to his son may well meet this criterion if the son is deprived of the love and attention normally expected from a father.

5. *Addictive behavior takes priority over all other life issues.* Addicts place their addiction at the center of their lives, and everything else revolves around it. It determines their lifestyle, their recreation (or lack of it), where they go, what they do. The gambling addict, for example, plans all her life around one theme: "When can I get into that next game?" "How can I work that casino into my travel plans?"

6. *Addicts deny their addiction.* That is, an addict denies the control the addiction has over him or her ("I can quit any time I like!") or the destructive consequences of the addictive ("It really doesn't hurt anybody," or "This one time won't hurt!")—even when these things are perfectly clear to others.

I recall challenging my younger brother many years ago about his smoking. "You're killing yourself," I told him. "You'll die of heart disease—or worse still, like Mom did." (Our mother, a heavy smoker, had died of lung cancer.)

"I think you are really addicted," I added, hoping to challenge him into changing.

"I can quit anytime I like," was his reply.

"I dare you," I countered.

He tried. Two days later he gave up. I was right—he was addicted. (I say "was" because his heart attack four years ago forced him to quit. It took the shock of a major illness to make him face up to his addiction and begin to overcome it.)

Recovery from an addiction cannot begin until this initial denial is broken. Even then, it may continue to reassert itself. Recovery from an addiction is a continual process of breaking through denial.

7. *In a sense, all addictions are substance addictions.* Recent research shows that eating disorders, preoccupation with certain sexual practices, workaholism, compulsive confessing, persistent thrill seeking or risk taking, and the compelling urge to feel wonderful have yet another factor in common with traditional addictions to alcohol, cocaine, narcotics, and other external substances. I believe it is this: *Both substance addictions and process addictions* may be caused by the body's tendency to become "hooked" on chemicals. In this sense, all addictions may eventually come to be seen as substance addictions.

In classic drug addictions, the chemicals that give pleasure (either as stimulants or tension-reducers) and cause destruction come from outside the body; they are called exogenous. In process addictions, the chemicals are possibly generated within the body: they are endogenous.

There are, of course, significant differences between the two. Substance addictions are clearly destructive, for example, whereas the damage done by addiction to internal chemicals may be less obvious. And there are significant differences in the mechanisms of onset and maintenance.

But despite these differences, there is a growing belief among scientists that activities become addicting because they stimulate the release of certain biochemicals and thus create a physical or emotional state the addict finds agreeable. The world's most prolific manufacturer and user of drugs is the brain itself. Thoughts, feelings, pain, pleasure, and even the emotional response to the so-called "recreational drugs" are mediated by chemical messengers manufactured in the brain! This is an important point often overlooked by those who insist that an addiction must be related to an external chemical substance.

The release of adrenaline in "emergencies," for instance, has long been known to be stimulating and, for many, pleasurable. And the relatively recent discovery that the brain manufactures its own opiatelike "endorphins" (short for "endogenous morphine") that serve to reduce pain and induce calmness has added credence (some would say final proof) to this understanding of how certain behaviors can be addicting.

The fact that we experience extreme physical discomfort, often resembling the withdrawal symptoms of drug addiction, when we abstain from certain activities points to the possibility that many behavior addictions have an underlying chemical basis. My clinical observation of high-pressured executives, for example, is that weekends and the first days of vacations can produce a physical letdown similar to the withdrawal symptoms of many drugs. (As a "recovering" Type-A personality, I've also experienced this myself.) And I—along with other clinicians—believe that this tension, restlessness, and nervous activity brought on in certain individuals by periods of idleness is due to the withdrawal effects of lowered adrenaline and other stress hormones.

In addition to withdrawal symptoms, "tolerance effects" (ever-increasing demands) are also noted in certain addictive behaviors. After a period of excitement—say, that of buying a new car—the system craves more excitement. Compulsive shopping is often associated with this need to seek a higher state of pleasurable arousal because the previous levels soon seem too ordinary and mundane.

The fact that brain chemistry may mediate mood does *not* remove personal responsibility for the activity that produces it. If anything, this connection between the brain and the feelings may *increase* responsibility. If *thoughts* can trigger the release of brain chemicals and thus play an important role in bringing on addictions, many addictions can therefore be thought of as self-induced and self-perpetuated. This of course points us back to issues of control and responsibility.

Once the addicting pattern has been established, however, the issue changes. While thoughts may trigger addiction, established addictions cannot be easily broken by thoughts or "willpower" alone. Overcoming addictions almost always requires guidance, support, and—in my opinion—the overcoming power of the Holy Spirit.

8. *All addictions involve psychological dependence.* Even if all addictions involve attachment to a chemical—either internal or external—experts agree that in an addiction the attachment is *not* purely physical: *In any addiction, psychological dependence is just as important as—or more important—than physical dependence.*

Researchers who study substance addictions are increasingly aware that dependence on an addicting substance transcends the physical need for it. In May, 1988, for example, *The Journal of Abnormal Psychology* published a special issue of "Models of Addiction" that summarized our present understanding of how substance addictions take place. In the opening editorial, Dr. Timothy B. Baker of the

University of Wisconsin at Madison concluded his review of our best scientific understanding of the addiction problem with the statement:

> ... "addiction" occurs in the *milieu externe,* not in the *milieu interne.* Addiction occurs in the environment, not in the liver, genes, or synapse.[4]

This is a powerful conclusion. It acknowledges that *much more* happens when someone becomes addicted to an external substance than just that substance's effects on the brain, liver, and other organs. While external substances *do* exert an influence on certain body systems, we cannot explain addictions *only* by these effects. There is much more going on.

For example, the ritual of injecting heroin or cocaine into a vein should not be understood merely as a means of avoiding the discomfort of withdrawal symptoms. Addicts are not "doing" these drugs just to avoid withdrawal symptoms; they have also developed a psychological dependence on the ritual of taking the drugs.

This is one reason readdiction in detoxified substance abuse patients can take place so rapidly. In other words, even someone whose body no longer has a craving for a drug can *much more rapidly* become readdicted because the psychological pleasure of the ritual has been established and is craved for its own sake. (Smokers who quit know this phenomenon well. Even though their bodies no longer crave the nicotine, they often long for the "ritual" of lighting up and holding the cigarette.)

The fact that even hardcore addictions have their psychological components makes it easier to understand how emotional habits and behaviors can become addicting. If a cocaine user is hooked by the "ritual" of preparing and taking the drug *as well as* by the drug itself, then it is very possible that any other ritual or activity can also become addicting *if* the pleasure associated with it is powerful enough.

My statement that hidden behaviors may well involve dependence on an internal chemical but that addictions to external chemicals involve psychological dependence may sound contradictory or confusing at first. Humans are very complex beings, and the relationship between body and mind cannot be reduced to simple categories. According to the latest research, most addictions seem to involve both chemical and psychological dependency. Effective treatment, therefore, must take both of these factors into account. I will discuss this in more depth in later chapters.

CATEGORIES OF ADDICTIONS

Addictions can be categorized in a number of ways. We could, for instance, group together those addictions that are *learned* and separate them from addictions that arise because of *deficiencies*. Compulsive gambling would be a *learned* addiction, whereas a craving for a particular food (or in some cases even alcohol) could be considered to be a *deficiency*, in the sense that the body craves something it doesn't have.

Still another way of categorizing addictions is according to the purpose or need they fulfill for the addict. As I have reflected for a number of years on the problem of addiction, I prefer to think of addictions as falling into the following classes:

• addictions that *stimulate,*
• addictions that *tranquilize,*
• addictions that serve some *psychological need,* and
• addictions that satisfy *unique appetites.*

It is important to realize that these categories overlap, and many addictions could fit in more than one category.

Compulsive gambling, for example, could *begin* as an activity that stimulates, that provides excitement and arousal, but could later come to fill the gambler's psychological need to control someone else or to prove his or her self-worth by "beating the odds." No single category of addiction can account for all the facets of a particular addiction. We need to keep this "multidimensional" understanding of addiction in mind at all points throughout the following discussion. It has important implications for our understanding and especially our treatment of the addictions.

Addictions That Stimulate. This category, which accounts for many common hidden addictions, would include addictions to activities that provide *arousal* and *ecstasy*. The body and the mind, working in unison, can be stimulated through a variety of mechanisms to produce pleasurable feelings to which a person can become addicted. Although these "mechanisms of stimulation" may have strong biochemical underpinnings, they are triggered primarily through psychological factors. In other words, we achieve the release of the body's internal "stimulant" chemistry by certain thought processes—such as rising to a challenge to be competitive in business, becoming argumentative, or "psyching ourselves up" for a game.

The form of stimulation I and many other "Type-A personalities" are familiar with is that great feeling of exhilaration we get when we "pump adrenaline." I can create an adrenaline "rush" just by getting caught up in some exciting project. Sleep goes by the board and other interests are pushed aside as I pursue the project. And it feels so good! I come alive with energy and I seem not to get tired.

This, of course, is what adrenaline is all about. It is the body's "emergency" hormone, and sooner or later it demands payment for its services. As we will see in a later chapter, adrenaline addiction increases the "wear and tear" on the body, and the price we pay when we become addicted to it is *stress disease.*

Addictions That Tranquilize. At the other end of the scale are those addictions that serve to tranquilize us. In this category we can include anything that *calms us, reduces nervous tension,* or *lowers anxiety.* In fact, any activity that makes us feel serene and tranquil *also* has the capacity to "hook" us. I believe that addictions to overeating and to certain types of food (such as carbohydrates and fats) fall into this category. So do addictions to certain sports and physical activities such as long-distance running.

On the whole, addictions that tranquilize tend not to be so physically destructive as addictions that stimulate. But they can be just as difficult to break, and they are far from harmless. An eating addiction, for instance, carries with it both physical risks (high blood pressure, heart disease, joint stress) and psychological ones (social condemnation for being obese, self-condemnation for being "out of control").

This form of addiction, like the others, probably has a basis in the chemistry of the brain. It has become quite clear in recent years that the brain has its own natural system of tranquilizers. In fact, the reason artificial tranquilizers such as Valium and Xanax, or painkillers such as morphine, work the way they do is that they mimic the activity of certain naturally produced substances. The best-known of these natural tranquilizers are called "endorphins." I will discuss these in more depth later in the book, but for now I simply want to point out that natural brain hormones play a major role in regulating our tranquillity and protecting us from pain. Because they can make us feel good, however, they have the capacity to "hook" us. Therefore any activity that stimulates their production in the brain can also be addicting.

We have only just begun to understand how these

hormones are triggered or inhibited and how certain behaviors can affect them. For instance, long-distance runners experience a "runner's high" at a certain stage in their exertion when large amounts of endorphin are spontaneously released (presumably to protect the body from the pain of pushing it to the limit). I am convinced that endorphins and other natural brain tranquilizers play a role in many hidden addictions. In such cases, the "payoff" for the behavior—the "pleasure factor"—is reduced tension and greater tranquillity. The years ahead will reveal many exciting discoveries as researchers push back the frontiers of our knowledge of how the brain works its miracles, every moment of every day.

Addictions That Serve Some Psychological Need. As I have shown, we cannot account for every hidden addiction solely on the basis of physiological dependence or brain biochemistry. Psychological factors also play a part. These, I suppose, can in turn be explained by reducing their mechanisms to submicroscopic biochemical interactions—and it is of course possible that in the future we will find even closer interconnections between mind and body.

I am convinced, however, from my extensive reading in this topic as well as my clinical experience that physiological factors cannot account altogether for human learning, longings, and the quest for meaningfulness. The mind is more than a brain. It is aware of feelings and seeks a purpose in life. Psychological mechanisms may have underlying biological support systems, but they also exist in their own right outside of the mechanics that make them work—in fact, they can change the way they work! This is the mystery of the human soul.

This means, then, that when a certain behavior meets some significant *psychological* need, the person will tend to repeat the behavior. If the behavior is harmful and the need very strong, an addiction can result.

Examples of addictions that meet psychological needs are a striving to achieve power, to overcome feelings of inadequacy, to prove one's self-worth, or even to engage in self-punishment. One particular type of addiction that can embrace all of these is workaholism.

Workaholism can have a very strong psychological component in that it can be a way of overcoming feelings of inadequacy or of achieving power. Obsessional tendencies (not obsessional disorders—these are quite different) can result from a need to engage in self-punishment, and relationship problems can have underlying needs rooted in previous rejection, insecurity, or inadequate parenting.

This category of hidden addiction is probably the most easily abused, with the most instances of erroneous labeling. As we proceed, I will try to set some limits on what constitutes a true addiction of this sort.

Addictions That Satisfy Unique Appetites. This is perhaps the most contentious category of all. For many years, researchers have tried to find a single, comprehensive theory that would account for *all* types of addiction. The most persistent theory, especially for alcoholism, is that there is a genetically determined "predisposition" to addiction. This means, in essence, that an individual inherits some special craving for the addictive substance or some particular way of reacting to it. Alcoholics, for instance, are considered to be different from nonalcoholics in either the route taken by the alcohol metabolism (the way the body disposes of the alcohol) or in the capacity to consume larger amounts of alcohol for longer periods than nonalcoholics. No definitive proof of this theory has yet been found, but a belief that there *are* differences between people who become alcoholic and those who don't persists.

The problem is complicated, as we will see, by the fact that an addiction of any sort always involves psychological as well as physiological factors. But it nevertheless appears to me that some sort of craving or "appetite" for a particular substance or feeling may be the basis for some addiction. Some of these appetites are probably common to most humans; how else can you explain the almost universal appeal of chocolate or ice cream? But other appetites may be limited to just a few.

For instance, I have noticed that I have absolutely no appetite for anything alcoholic. In fact, my unique taste buds dislike it quite intensely. Yet I know others who crave the taste quite strongly, even though they seldom drink anything alcoholic. This may partly be explained by differences in background—if you are exposed to a substance very early in life, you might learn to like it more than if you are only exposed to it later—but I doubt if this adequately explains all our differences in appetites.

I remain convinced, therefore, that some addictions have their origins in unique appetites that may differ from person to person. These appetites may be determined by a unique combination of sensory perception (through genetic factors), a unique conditioning of the senses (through early learning in which a taste for a particular substance is created), or perhaps even by some deficiency in the body that sets up a physical craving for the substance. We may crave certain foods, for instance, simply because the body needs the particular nutrients the food provides. Such a craving, then, can be the basis upon which an addiction is built. We will explore the issue of cravings further in the next chapter and show both how they can lead to addiction and how the addiction reinforces them.

WHAT CREATES A NEED FOR ADDICTIVE BEHAVIOR?

It may be decades before we fully understand the complex relationship of body and mind in maintaining an addiction. But whether addiction is more a physical dependence or a psychological one, certain fundamental psychological needs clearly underlie addictive behavior. All of us, in fact, are capable of some addictive behavior, because we all have these needs. This is the nature of being human: We are imperfect and come into adulthood with certain psychological "hungers" that we constantly seek to feed.

But in our attempt to meet these deficiencies or correct these flaws we can easily get caught up in behaviors that are self-defeating or blot out our awareness of even deeper needs. It is these behaviors that lay the foundation for addiction bonds.

What are the major psychological needs that contribute to an addictive process?

- a need to escape from worry and anxiety,
- a need to reduce guilt feelings,
- a need for a sense of control and power in one's environment,
- a need to avoid pain (physical, psychological, and spiritual),
- a need to have order and be free of confusion,
- a need to be a "perfect" person:
  —a quest for the perfect self
  —a quest for perfect health
  —a quest for perfect personality
  —a quest for perfect performance.

I have said that the one central theme in all addictions, whether hidden addictions or the more obvious chemical addictions, is their function of removing us from full awareness and experience of our true, deepest feelings. Most, if not all, addicts have feelings they cannot tolerate. These feelings are so painful that the person seeks protection from them; the addictive behavior places a buffer between the addict and the painful feelings.

We readily see this in the case of alcohol addiction. The

alcoholic finds life too painful to endure "head on," so he or she turns to alcohol to tranquilize the pain and obliterate the feelings related to that pain.

But what about the workaholic? Or the compulsive shopper? Or the addictive overeater? Do these addictions serve the same purpose? Very much so. Whether the addiction serves to stimulate us or sedate our pain, the final effect is to rob us of our true feelings.

What are some of the feelings we run away from?

- We can't tolerate *boredom*—so we seek stimulation and provocation.
- We can't tolerate *humdrum routine*—so we seek stimulation and provocation.
- We can't tolerate *depression*—so we seek escape and relief.
- We can't tolerate *feeling inadequate*—so we seek a sense of power, mastery, and control.
- We can't tolerate *feeling imperfect*—so we seek a perfect body and mind.
- We can't tolerate *low self-esteem*—so we seek a sense of self-mastery and self-aggrandizement.
- We can't tolerate *stress*—so we seek tranquillity and escape.

Because the basic drive in addiction is to avoid painful feelings and experiences, anything that masks these feelings can become an "addictive" cover or escape. There is one complicating factor, however: the buildup of *tolerance*. Over time, the addictive behavior becomes less effective at blocking the feelings we want to avoid—so we have to ingest the substance or practice the behavior again and again, more and more often, in order to achieve the desired effect.

This is the trap of all addictions. It is here that the potential for sin is very great. Addicts of all sorts eventually become imprisoned by their addictive behavior, and the emotional chains which are forged are as powerful as the strongest steel. Whereas they start by offering freedom from the inevitable pain of life, they slowly become a prison because the pleasure they offer is temporary.

Sooner or later, the workaholic has to face times of idleness, and the sexual addict must confront the mundane reality of life without sexual stimulation. In this respect, people with hidden addictions are no different from the alcoholic who has to wake up to a new day of reality with a hangover.

Addictions are a problem, then, not only because they involve harmful behavior, but because, in the long run, *they don't deliver what they purportedly promise.* There is *no* escape from life; it must be lived in stark reality—but with the confidence and resilience that God gives us as we entrust our lives (and feelings) to him.

WHAT ABOUT PERSONAL RESPONSIBILITY?

Approaching the problem of addiction—and especially the "hidden" addictions—inevitably involves the question of personal *responsibility* and, with it, the question of choice. Timothy Baker, quoted earlier in this chapter, stresses that "an individual chooses to take drugs in the world" even though "the likelihood of a person trying a drug or eventually becoming addicted *is influenced* by his or her friends, marital happiness, the variety and richness of alternatives to drug use, and so on."[5]

So even though an external substance may cause an addiction, *we still remain morally responsible for what we do and the choices we make.* If this is true for substance abuse, it is certainly true for our "hidden addictions." Alcoholics Anonymous (AA) and other successful recovery groups have consistently taken the approach of holding the addict morally responsible. AA groups, in fact, can sometimes be almost brutal in their indictment of "excuse making" and "blame shifting." Their entire program rests on the addicts' owning their problem and taking responsibility for their choices.

The question of personal responsibility, however, points to an even deeper issue, a spiritual one. At bottom, addictions of all sorts are fundamentally a manifestation of a more basic problem, that basic spiritual and moral deficiency that goes by the general name *sin.*

Keith Miller makes this point very powerfully in his provocative book, *Sin: Overcoming the Ultimate Deadly Addiction.* While his main thrust is on the addictive power of *sin* itself and on how it affects every aspect of the Christian life, he also points to human sin as the unseen "disease" beneath all other addictions: "It's as if beneath the addictive behaviors there is some unseen cause in the life of the addicted person; it is this underlying cause that is the real root cause [of the addiction]."[6]

Our bondage to a persistent and problematic behavior is, in the final analysis, a *bondage to sin.* We must not overlook the spiritual dimensions of our addictions, and we need help in making the right choices at the right time. Much of this help can come from psychological insights and healing—but not all of it.

Fortunately, as we will see, God has not left us destitute and helpless, but "he will show you how to escape temptation's power so that you can bear up patiently against it" (1 Cor 10:13 LB). Addictive disorders represent disorders of self-control. We need help from outside ourselves in establishing this control.

TWO

Addictions and Cravings

T OM IS ADDICTED TO WORRYING.
That's not what I thought when I first saw him pro-
fessionally; I thought he was a workaholic. But as he and I
explored his problem in more depth, I realized that although
he worked very hard and liked to make money, he wasn't
addicted to either work or money. Instead, Tom was a
"worryholic." Not surprisingly, the *content* of his worry (*what*
he worried about) was not important. He could worry about
anything—whether he was wearing the right colored socks
to whether a space shuttle launch would go O.K. You name
it—he could turn it into worry. It was the *process* of worrying
itself that had him hooked.

Tom used all his spare time to worry; he even kept a
notebook of things that bothered him. Usually this helps a
person to "let go" of the worry, but Tom used it as additional
memory! Even when things were going right and he was
extremely successful, he would dream up situations to stew
over.

Why did Tom have this urge to worry? In many respects it
seemed that he "craved" worrying, just as I might "crave"
ice cream. It will be a long time before we completely unravel
the complex biochemistry and psychology of how such
craving develops, and that it can exist for processes like

worrying as well as for substances like food or drugs. All we can see is the outward behavior that somehow provides inner satisfaction. In Tom's case, that behavior was worry. In some strange way, he felt safer, calmer, when he was worrying. It reset some inner urge and quieted the restless storm within. By worrying about a possible catastrophe, he irrationally believed he was in fact preventing the catastrophe from happening.

(I have encountered such "magic" thinking often in Christians who develop a habit I call "worry praying." They pray constantly, but not in the biblical sense in which we are to be prayerful at all times. Rather, the repetitive prayer is employed to somehow "force" God into preventing the catastrophe they fear. This form of praying, when engaged in habitually, is an expression of "worry anxiety," not faith, and it may easily become an addiction.)

For Tom, periods free of worry created first a restlessness, then a low-grade depression—seemingly a type of "withdrawal." It set up a craving to worry, outwardly similar to a craving one gets for some substance. When he was worrying, however, his body and mind went into action, triggering a "fight or flight" response—an increase in the level of adrenaline and other stress hormones—that renewed his sense of control. Worry, in essence, created a state of arousal for Tom that made him feel better. It was the return to a nonaroused state—with lowered levels of stress hormones—that Tom found so unpleasant, not the times of worrying.

The process of healing was a slow one for Tom. It took many hours of prayer and counseling, along with the support of a loving wife, to teach him what it felt like to be normal. Tom had to learn how to tolerate lowered adrenaline arousal and even how to see boredom and peacefulness as friends and not enemies.

I am pleased to report that after two years of determined effort, Tom can now appreciate how wonderful it is to be free of worry. In a sense, however, he will never be completely "cured." In all addictions, once the mind and the body have created an appetite or craving for a particular state or substance, "hunger pangs" for the state or substance will frequently reemerge. This is why alcoholics will always label themselves as alcoholics, even when they've been sober for fifty years. In process addictions as well, the hard truth is: once an addict—always an addict. The substance or habit may be gone, but the basic craving for it will always be there.

Now my point in telling Tom's story is to show that "cravings" are not just food or drug related. To understand how process or hidden addictions begin and continue, therefore, it helps to have a basic understanding of cravings. To have an addiction means you crave something. So, what is craving? How does it develop and what maintains it? These questions cannot be overlooked if you are to avoid developing an addiction.

WHAT IS A CRAVING?

The term *craving* has generally been considered to be unscientific because it is subjective and difficult to define. Nevertheless, it is a term that keeps coming up in describing addictions[1] and can be helpful in understanding them.

In lay terms, a craving is simply a strong desire for something, such as a food or drink. We all experience cravings from time to time. Ask someone a simple question like "What do you crave?" and almost everyone has an immediate answer. Most people, for example, know what it's like to have an overwhelming desire for an apple, chocolate, or a milkshake.

I recall that once during my high school years, right in the middle of a year-end examination, I was overcome by a powerful and almost uncontrollable craving for ice cold milk. The room was hot and I was frustrated with the long examination. My taste buds went into some crazy agitation that in my mind could only be satisfied by very cold milk. I clearly recall enduring the agony of that two-hour test, then rushing home and almost demolishing the refrigerator handle in my haste to get at the milk. To my dismay the refrigerator was empty! I rode my bicycle as fast as I could to the local store, bought a quart of the coldest milk I could find, and guzzled it right there in the shop. But what was I really craving? Was I just thirsty or did my body need a specific substance because of a deficiency? Was it perhaps some deep need to be succored by milk—a return to my mother's breast?

These are intriguing questions and they do increase my fascination for understanding the physiology and psychology (or in technical terms the "neurobiology") of craving. Unfortunately the experts are not yet agreed on any unified theory of cravings, let alone its impact on addiction. Frankly, we just don't know how cravings are formed. Some have tried to confine it to physical desires, believing that the psychological aspects of craving cannot be measured adequately and can easily be falsified—so who can know the truth? Others insist that cravings are *not* just physical but heavily depend on "psychic" or "psychological" factors as well. I believe this. Not only do cravings arise because of fundamental needs like eating, sleeping, and sex, but also because we need love, a purpose for existing, and personal fulfillment. So while at the physical level, cravings can be explained as electrical stimulation of fibers within a certain part of the forebrain that powerfully reinforces certain behaviors, these stimulations do not represent all cravings. It is possible that aspirations and feelings can also set up equal, if not more powerful, cravings.

There are many other kinds of cravings. Many people also crave new experiences or a repeat of some previous pleasurable event. Whether the craving is for a substance or an experience, everyone is familiar with the discomfort—

sometimes, the agony—that is felt until the urge is satisfied or the mind is distracted by other thoughts. Psychologists universally agree that people can be driven by, and are motivated to satisfy, their cravings and stop the discomfort that these unsatisfied urges engender.

Such an urge to satisfy a craving may well be the root of an addiction. And addictions, once established, are maintained partially by the discomfort of the cravings.

Not all cravings result in addiction, of course—nor do all addictions begin with cravings. The only thing we can be certain of is that cravings are a by-product of living—a given of life. Whether a craving becomes an addiction or not will depend on other factors.

The human body cannot survive without some cravings. Sometimes it will set up a craving for a specific food because it lacks a nutrient or energy source. The physical *need* creates a craving with its accompanying discomfort. (This is probably the reason pregnant women, with their changing physical needs, sometimes experience powerful and unusual cravings.) In normal needs this cycle of craving/ satisfaction is harmless, almost necessary.

At other times the craving is created by a *memory* of something highly pleasant. For example, I love to travel, and I have a particular partiality for Switzerland, Austria, and southern Germany, especially Bavaria. The thought of these places triggers deep and pleasant feelings in me. I love the scenery, but also the people, the smells, the architecture, the music. Every now and then I am overcome with a craving to visit one of these places. It's not as if I have been there often; I have visited only once or twice. But these places resonated with a deep part of me, perhaps because in my early adult years I loved to read about them. My memory of those books and my visits is enough to establish a craving to travel to that part of Europe again.

When I feel the urge to visit one of these places I am always struck with the strength of the feeling. Distraction and a busy life schedule soon diminish it, but not without a brief period of discomfort during which I assure myself that an opportunity to travel to these beautiful places will come again some day. In any case, the intense craving for travel is not at all unpleasant. In fact, I quite enjoy the fantasizing about it. I love to re-live previous travels and to plan future ones. I suppose such a craving could be destructive if I allowed it to create a high level of frustration.

Cravings, then, are neither good nor bad in themselves. They involve a certain discomfort, but they are not always unpleasant. They serve the purpose of maintaining the body's balance of "homeostasis." A craving is created when a need arises—and satisfying the need restores the mind and body to peace. It is how we respond to the craving that determines whether or not it becomes harmful. Many addictions, then, have their origins in cravings that can no longer be controlled. This is true for substances—it is also true for behaviors.

HOW CRAVINGS BECOME ADDICTIONS

Where does a craving stop and an addiction begin? A craving becomes an addiction when one *cannot control one's response to it*. A craving is simply a strong desire for something; an addiction is the inability to *stop oneself from fulfilling the desire*. In addiction the craving becomes reinforced (positively or negatively) in such a way that the body and mind becomes dependent on it. The craving cycle is thus beyond reasonable control by the addict. The craving also becomes insatiable. No matter how many times you partake of something you can't seem to get enough of it. When a craving has been indulged, the satisfaction is short-lived; very quickly a new cycle of craving and discomfort begins again. In a way, then, an addiction can be seen as a cycle of unsatisfied cravings or the natural process of craving gone haywire. The need seems to outrun one's capacity to satisfy the need.

Sometimes the satisfaction an addict experiences after responding to a craving is far in excess of what can be accounted for by the activity or behavior. There is greater pleasure or relief than can be explained by the behavior. This can also become the basis for an addiction.

This "exaggerated response" is often seen in a severe compulsive behavior. (Such a disorder is not an addiction, as explained in chapter 11, but the mechanism of out-of-proportion response is similar.) A victim of a compulsive disorder may feel compelled to perform a little ritual, such as tapping a doorknob several times before opening the door. Usually this starts because the person is very anxious about going into a room. The irrational belief emerges that if you tap the doorknob, in some magical way everything will become all right. The habit soon becomes a craving—a craving for freedom from anxiety. So it becomes a ritual that is performed again and again.

This is an excessive "pay-off" for a simple action. The satisfaction is out of all proportion to the nature of the behavior—a simple tap on the door handle. But this illustrates the tremendous power that psychological mechanisms and simple behaviors can have over us. When a behavior has this sort of power it is in all respects equivalent to an addiction to any powerful drug—it can certainly disrupt or even destroy one's life.

PARALLELS BETWEEN SUBSTANCE AND PROCESS ADDICTIONS

Our limited understanding of how cravings work has revealed some fascinating facets of how addictions begin and maintain themselves. And as I have indicated in chapter 1, much of what has been discovered about substance addictions also has a parallel in the hidden or process addictions.

This doesn't surprise me. After all, since process addictions may also involve biochemical changes, they must be seen as chemical addictions in a sense. (The body cannot tell whether a substance enters through the mouth or nostril or whether it comes from some internal gland or the brain.) In addition, the mind, with its complex learning ability and fantastic memory circuits, is capable of being programmed by pleasure-seeking of all sorts. We will see later how this "memory" for addiction goes far beyond the body's biological dependence on a substance.

Because of space limitations I will focus here on *three* parallels between substance and process addictions that can help us develop our understanding of how addictive cravings are reinforced and hopefully, how addicted people can be released from them.

"Classes" of Addictions. It is generally recognized that habit-forming substances fall into two groups, classified according to the way they reinforce behavior. The similarities in effect seem to be due to the fact that a given class of substance activates a particular neuronal circuit in the brain.[2]

First, there are those drugs that provide *positive reinforcement.* Here the drug provides a "high" or euphoric state to a person who is in a normal state of mind and level mood. Cocaine, amphetamines, and nicotine are examples of this kind of drug. The caffeine in coffee or cola drinks would also fall into this class, generally known as *stimulants.*

Second, there are those substances that provide *negative reinforcement.* Here the drug terminates distress and *returns* the person to normal. These substances, known as *sedatives,* include alcohol, barbiturates, opiates, and the benzodiazepines (minor tranquilizers). Substances that set up severe physical withdrawal symptoms (such as heroin or alcohol) also falls into this second class because it, too, provides *negative* reinforcement. The addiction arises partly as a way of avoiding the painful withdrawal symptoms.

It is important to understand that drugs like cocaine, amphetamines, and nicotine are addicting because of the *positive* reinforcement they provide, not just because of any withdrawal symptoms. This distinction is important and also applies to different classes of process addictions. It is also important to note that the socially accepted drugs such as alcohol, caffeine, and nicotine can activate the same neuronal circuits as "hard" drugs such as heroin.

The fact that drugs fall into two distinct classes and that within each class they have common characteristics may have very important parallels in the hidden addictions. If different drugs involve different parts of the brain, then different process addictions may also be connected with different brain functions. Those that provide *positive* reinforcement affect one part of the brain, those that provide *negative* reinforcement, another.

Simple observation of behavior supports this idea. Some behaviors clearly serve to stimulate and arouse us, using *positive reinforcement* to give us a "lift." Examples of such behaviors might be constant high-pressure or deadline work, (as in workaholism), thrill seeking (as in riding roller coasters, sky diving, racing automobiles), or gambling. Other behaviors serve the purpose of calming us down when we are anxious or relieving our tension; acting as sedatives or tranquilizers to provide *negative reinforcement*. They include arguing (for some people at least), compulsive confessing, overeating, and excessive TV watching.

This is somewhat speculative, of course. And it is very possible that different behaviors may serve different purposes for different people. For example, some runners run for the excitement of competition; others say it "calms them down." Some people use sex as a tranquilizer; others as a source of stimulation. But my point is simply that process addictive behaviors do seem to work on specific circuits of the brain, thus falling into the same categories as substances.

Our "Memory" for Addictions. The second very significant parallel between substance and process addictions involves a fact that is obvious on reflection, but which often eludes the thinking of even experienced drug therapists: A substance addiction need *not* be rooted in the distress of withdrawal (the unpleasant feelings associated with the stopping of the addiction).[3] Some drugs (cocaine is a notable example) are highly addicting *without* having any unpleasant effects when they are stopped.

This has always puzzled therapists. If withdrawal is not the addicting mechanism, what *does* establish and maintain the addiction?

The answer is *memory!* The addict can *remember* the reinforcing effects of the addicting substance. Even without withdrawal symptoms, this memory of reinforcement is enough to create a craving and continue the addictive behavior. This memory, in essence, is essential to what we mean by "psychological dependence."

This psychological component accounts for the inadequacy of many drug-treatment programs that provide replacement drugs. Such therapy treats only the physical withdrawal symptoms associated with detoxification; it does not treat the "memory" of pleasure. And this residual memory leaves the addict vulnerable to readdiction long after the body is free of drugs. Now, if the brain can "remember" how pleasurable a drug felt and create a craving for more of it, then clearly it can also "remember" how pleasurable a behavior was and crave it also. If the behavior is also associated with a heightened internal arousal (such as heightened adrenaline), this memory can be extremely powerful. It creates a vicious addiction. Many people become hooked on perversion or sadistic behavior through this mechanism; in their minds, sex becomes linked with the heightened stimulation of danger or forbidden activity.

I am not suggesting that all process addictions depend solely on the memory of the addictive behavior's pleasure-giving properties. But memory is certainly a powerful contributing factor, and it may be a far more important mechanism of control than we have hitherto realized. I believe it will need to receive greater attention in the future if we are to gain control over our destructive behaviors.

The "Crossover" Effect of Craving. The realization that drugs fall into two distinct classes (stimulants and sedatives) and that memory for pleasure plays a powerful role in establishing an addiction leads us to the third and perhaps the most important observation: There is a very significant "crossover" effect among drugs in the same category. Since both nicotine and caffeine are stimulant drugs, taking *either* one of them stimulates the same neurochemical circuits. If the smoker tries to stop smoking while continuing to drink strong coffee, therefore, the craving for both will be maintained. Alternatively, a person who gives up smoking and then replaces it with drinking strong coffee is only substituting another stimulant, not breaking an addiction to stimulants. And this "crossover" effect applies to many of the major drugs as well. It may well be, for example, that coffee drinking may maintain a cocaine addiction.

But what about our hidden addictions? Are they subject to the same "crossover"? I believe they are. Gambling and mountaineering, for instance, may be interchangeable for some people because both are positive reinforcers and act as stimulants. Excessive TV watching and overeating may be interchangeable because they are both negative reinforcers, serving to calm us down or help us avoid pain.

Once again, the *reason* these activities can be interchanged is that they affect the brain in similar ways—activating the same neuronal circuits. In the case of high-risk behavior, for example, it is not the activity itself that causes the addiction, but the danger associated with it. Your addiction may be cliff climbing, but you could substitute hang-gliding, diving off a high cliff into the ocean, or aerobatic flying and feel a similar effect. All such activities are clearly in the stimulant class of behaviors; they stimulate the body's survival mechanism. In the face of danger, the heart pumps adrenaline through every muscle and nerve, preparing the body to fight for survival. Many people find this state of heightened adrenaline highly pleasurable; their addiction is actually to this state of arousal.

I believe this "crossover" of behaviors needs to be better understood. Without taking it into account in recovery from an addiction, we may simply end up trading one addiction for another.

CONCLUSIONS ABOUT CRAVINGS

What important lessons can we learn from this exploration of how cravings work in both substance and process addictions?

1. *We need to guard against developing an addiction to any class of substances or behaviors because of the far-reaching impact of such an addiction.* Even activities that seem good and harmless in themselves can be devastating if allowed to develop into addictions. Workaholism, for example, may seem to pay dividends in early life, bringing financial rewards and business success, but it carries heavy personal and family penalties over the long haul.

2. *In trying to give up a particular addiction, we should carefully consider whether we should give up other behaviors that are in the same "class."* It's also a good idea to consider giving up minor drugs that serve the same purpose as certain behaviors. For example, drinking large quantities of coffee or smoking while trying to control a stimulating behavior is likely to be self-defeating.

3. *Healing of addictions must involve psychological processes as well as physical ones.* Since the memory of highly pleasurable activities can be *a powerful* source of cravings, we should remember that addictions are much more than simple physical dependencies. The expectancy that pleasure is to be had in doing something is a very powerful force. The healing of our hidden addictions therefore lies very much in the realm of mending the distortions of our memory—or, in many cases, reversing and extinguishing the memory of the pleasure.

The exercise of *choice* is thus essential. It is important to throw out any hint that addicts "have no choice." All healing begins with an assertion of the "right to choose." We have to choose to stop doing certain things and to continue *not* doing them before the memory will give up its power to control us. Knowing that this takes time, and that abstinence is the best extinguisher, can help tremendously.

4. *Since addictions involve complex neurochemical reactions in the brain, they are very powerful and not easily overcome.* While a few are able to go "cold turkey" and by dint of willpower simply decide to stop a given behavior, most addicts will need lots of help to overcome their addiction.

Those who have never been enslaved by an irresistible urge to do something probably cannot appreciate the incredible force of the addictive urge. It can sometimes feel like a dozen bulldozers moving in unison to run over one's good intentions. Relying on one's own power is seldom successful in the long run.

Fortunately, relying on oneself is unnecessary. Both human and divine resources are abundantly available, and I will explore both in the chapters to come.

Addictions are indeed powerful and destructive, but God has not left us to our own devices in confronting them. He has promised us help in *every* time of trouble; no matter how severe the trial or temptation, there is a way of escape (1 Cor 10:13). He longs to empower us for effective living. The more we "go it alone," the more we grieve him.

Of course, it is one thing knowing that we can turn to God for help and another more difficult matter to actually do it. I will attempt to give more specific help on how to do this in the final chapter of this book.

5. *In the final analysis, our cravings for pleasure or escape or our hunger for certain experiences must be seen as a search for meaning and purpose in this life.* For many, it is the lure of escape from the harshness of reality. For others it is the premature experience of a grossly inadequate "touch of heaven." The search for ecstasy, whether through cocaine, sex, or sky-diving, is an attempt to sample heaven—and it fails horribly because nothing on earth has the power to give us that experience. Only God's heaven promises eternal ecstasy!

In the last analysis, our struggle with all addictions is a struggle to live fully and meaningfully. Giving ourselves over to any addiction—no matter how positive or harmless the addicting activity is in itself—may keep us from discovering that real life, fully lived, with our feet solidly grounded in God's reality, may be the best preparation there is for our heavenly experience later.

It is my prayer that as you continue to read and confront your own hidden addictions you will be able, with God's empowerment, to set them aside in favor of achieving a fuller life. Make no mistake; it is hard work. One of the attractions of all addictions is that they promise a "short-cut" to happiness and "instant" gratification. There's no such thing! We will never know deep and abiding happiness unless we work to achieve it, nor will we ever be content with "basic" life while we repeatedly make excursions into the realm of ecstasy.

THREE

Is There an Addictive Personality?

B ERNARD WAS MY FRIEND MANY YEARS AGO. We were both about twelve or thirteen years of age when we became close friends, living a few blocks from each other and both going to the same school.

What was it that attracted me to Bernard? I have not seen or heard from him since we left school and went our separate ways, but I still remember him well. He was a "gadget person." He collected gadgets. He made gadgets. He invented gadgets. He never threw a gadget away. He was my kind of man.

Bernard hated school and formal learning, but he was brilliant with his hands. He never needed to read an instruction booklet when assembling something, nor did he need a repair manual for a bicycle, toaster, or anything else that needed fixing. Even at thirteen years of age, he understood how mechanical objects ticked.

I must confess I envied Bernard greatly, and I have even mimicked him somewhat in my own life by becoming a bit of a "gadget person" myself. I normally read the assembly instructions *after* I have put something together, more for the fun of seeing whether the manufacturer got it right than for learning anything.

But there was something about Bernard that intrigued me even more than his wide-ranging abilities: he seemed addicted to collecting broken leftover pieces. Of course, I never thought of it as "addiction" until recently, when I began to recall our relationship and relive some of our experiences. But I can see in retrospect that Bernard was hooked. He *never* threw anything away. Wire, screws, and nuts would "always come in handy." He had boxes of them. Too many for one lifetime. They cluttered his room and his parents' house. He had assembled a large assortment of spare parts and, most important of all, he was passionately caught up with his one preoccupation. I even suspected that he went to bed at night clutching some gadget in each arm. (He denied this, of course.)

His passion was totally captivating and to some degree destructive. His addiction intruded into the lives of others, and I deeply suspected that he did it not to be frugal but because his collection prevented him from facing life's realities.

Yes, Bernard loved fixing things—but more, he could never throw anything away. It obsessed him to the point that he was restless, irritable, edgy, and totally miserable if ever forced to part with some of his junk.

Now, what intrigues me about Bernard is that he had been that way ever since he could remember. Was it a part of his personality? What was the connection between his need to hold on to things and some deep inner conflict or insecurity? It seemed to me that his addiction to collecting leftover junk, not just an assortment of spare parts, was based on some hidden need, and that it helped him to cope with his painful emotions.

IS THERE AN ADDICTIVE PERSONALITY?

Since addiction is at heart an individual response of coping with unpleasant reality, two questions naturally arise: 1. Are certain individuals prone to develop certain addictions? 2. Is there a personality style common to all addictions?

Together, these two questions have far-reaching implications:

- for prevention of addictions, hidden or otherwise,
- for treatment and the development of treatment strategies,
- for understanding the role of personal responsibility in addictions.

Now the big question, of course, is what do we mean by *personality*? Many people use the word to mean the qualities (usually positive) of a person that leave their mark or impression on other people. "He's got a great personality," we might say about someone, meaning that he is outgoing, friendly, or entertaining. In this popular sense, personality is that nonphysical quality which attracts us to someone or repels us.

Psychologists, however, attach a more basic meaning to the word. They see personality as the total of those abiding qualities that make a person distinctive. It is the totality of mental and relational traits that uniquely sets one person apart from everyone else. Everyone, therefore, has a personality. We may be friendly and outgoing or shy and introverted. We may always be in a hurry, or we may be slow and methodical.

Personalities, then, can fall into different categories or "types," but the criteria for classifying them vary. Some approaches to classifying personality have focused on internal mechanisms of feeling, others on outward characteristics or behaviors. There is no universally accepted system for describing personality. However, we do at least agree on one point: everyone has a personality or *distinctive style* of relating to the world.

HOW PERSONALITY SHAPES SUBSTANCE ABUSE

Most of the research into the relationship between personality and addiction has been done in the area of substance addiction. Studies have indicated that personality is one of *three* factors that contribute to any problem of substance addiction; the others are environment, and the particular addictive substance[1] (see figure 1).

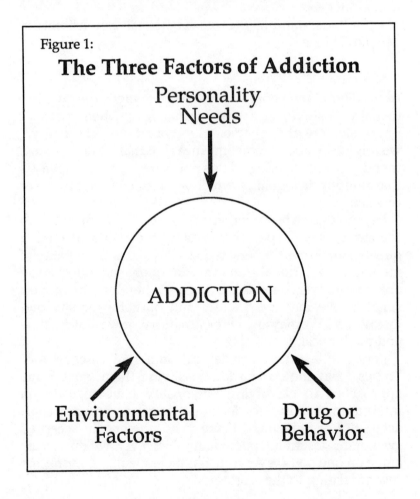

Figure 1:

The Three Factors of Addiction

Personality Needs

ADDICTION

Environmental Factors

Drug or Behavior

But while most experts agree that personality factors contribute significantly to the development of a substance addiction, the search for any *one* personality type that tends toward addiction has been discouraging. We have little evidence as yet that one type of person is more likely to become an addict than another. (It may be too early in the development of our understanding of the broader concept of addiction; perhaps one day we may have a more complete answer.)

As one examines the personality characteristics of substance addicts, however, several suggestive "threads" do emerge:

- Substance addicts tend to be nonconventional. (They are disaffected with religion, rebellious, and less driven by socially defined achievement goals.)
- They tend to be open to new experiences (sensation seeking, playful, and so on).
- They tend to seek immediate gratification of their needs and don't tolerate delays well.
- They tend to suffer from low self-esteem before becoming addicted.
- They tend to be alienated from traditional cultural values (especially drug addicts) usually because their addiction is shunned by others.

These "threads" are possibly the result of society's rejection of most illegal drugs. People addicted to prescription drugs, and some alcoholics tend not to have these qualities, because these substances are socially sanctioned.

This general list is far from conclusive, of course. And it is impossible to be any more conclusive—for instance, to link particular personality traits with particular addictions.

Several factors make the connection between personality and substance addiction particularly difficult to sort out:

1. *One difficulty is that there is a difference between an addictive*

personality and an addicted personality. The former refers to a predisposition to addiction while the latter to what the personality becomes after an addiction has taken hold. It is often very difficult to separate these two.

2. Another difficulty in distinguishing an addictive personality comes from the fact that *different people may become addicted to a given drug for different reasons—thus, different personalities may come to be addicted to the same drug.*

Take amphetamines, for instance. Amphetamines, a variety of stimulant drugs that easily become addictive, are taken for a variety of reasons. They suppress appetite, so overweight people sometimes use them for weight control. They also produce wakefulness, so students studying for exams, truck drivers on long hauls, and medical interns on call use them to keep from falling asleep. High doses of the amphetamines produce an intense, pleasurable "high," so some people take them just for the thrill.

The point is that addiction to one substance can grow out of any number of different needs and motivations. Substance addictions arise from different factors, and while personality may play an important role in setting up an individual addiction, *no one type of personality* can be shown to be more prone to a given addiction than another.

3. Yet another complication to this picture is presented by the fact that *what starts an addiction may not always be what keeps it going.* A chance exposure to a drug or challenge to "experiment" with it or both may be the first link in a long chain of addictive motivations. The first "motive" may simply be to be "one of the crowd." Later it shifts to reinforcing social needs as the addict begins to enjoy the social rituals associated with the addiction.

This can be clearly seen in the case of Marian, who developed a very common form of "hidden" alcoholism: that of the wife who is a secret drinker.

As a young woman, Marian never touched alcohol. She had despised her alcoholic mother and had vowed never to be like her. Several years after her second child was born, however, Marian began to drink secretly.

At the time, Marian felt lonely, rejected, and dissatisfied. Her husband was engrossed in his job as an engineer, and communication between them had deteriorated. Torn between staying at home to raise her children and going to work, she had opted for staying at home mainly because her husband insisted that a wife "should be a good home-maker." She stayed home not because she wanted to, but because she thought staying home would win her husband's respect.

Social drinking had become a part of their life—especially in recent years, when her husband had begun to insist that they socialize with his work buddies. So gradually Marian got over her dislike for alcohol. She also discovered that it "killed her worries." Very soon, during the long hours of loneliness and the boredom of the day, she would "liven" up her mood with a few drinks.

By the time Marian came for help, she was drinking every day, often to the point where she would be quite intoxicated when her husband came home from work. She had reached the point where she could not tolerate her pain without the help of alcohol.

But an interesting thing had also begun to happen. As Marian's drinking problem became evident, her husband had begun to show some concern. Sometimes he would actually came home earlier from work to "check up on her." Marian had soon found she could manipulate his caring for her by drinking to excess just before he came home. The underlying reason for the alcohol abuse had changed over time from relieving boredom to getting attention. It wasn't until the husband threatened to divorce her that she came to her senses and sought help.

The point here is that motives for an addiction—and accordingly, the personality factors that lead to an addiction—can change over time. Many aspects of the addiction can give pleasure or avoid pain, and many motivational "roots" are put down to support the growth of an addiction—whether this addiction is to substances or to behaviors. This means that in cases of substance abuse, it is the *psychological dependence* arising from these many motivations, not the physical dependence, which in the long run constitutes the main problem. Physical symptoms of withdrawal following abstinence can be distressing and even life-threatening, but they can be handled quite adequately with skilled supervision. Psychological dependence—and by this I mean the many motives and deep needs that are met by the addiction—is what makes an addiction resistant to treatment in the long run. Substance addictions have high relapse rates precisely because they are *not* simply physical addictions. They meet the same underlying needs as process addictions.

HOW PERSONALITY SHAPES PROCESS ADDICTIONS

Do the connections and complications between personality and substance addiction also apply to process abuse? As I have mentioned, most of what has been written applies only to substance addictions, but in my clinical experience some very clear patterns are emerging among process addicts.

1. The first of these—a quite startling revelation to me—is that *while some of the personality characteristics that predispose people to substance addiction are also common to process or behavior addictions, many of them are exactly the opposite.* Let me explain.

As I have indicated, substance addicts tend to be *nonconventional.* They are disillusioned with religion, the social order, and regular living styles. They want change and are less driven by socially defined achievement goals or ideas of "success."

This is the opposite of what I see in many people with

"hidden" addictions. These people seem to be very conventional and to have a great need for order. Workaholics, for example, are often driven by comparisons they make between themselves and others and are very much committed to the rat race for success. Compulsive gamblers are seldom "disengaged" from life. Obsessive runners are not running away from life but are often very much caught up in overcompliance; they tend to do everything by the book.

People who become substance addicts tend to be open to new experiences—perhaps because people who are open to new experiences are more likely to try drugs in the first place. For example, moderate student drug users are reported to be more open-minded, creative, flexible, adventurous, and less narrowly conventional.[2] They know how to play and have a "healthy regression in the service of the ego" as one researcher described it. In short, they know how to be childlike.

Granted, these comparisons are with only moderate drug users, not with addicts. Nevertheless, this description sounds to me like the opposite of what is typical for process addicts. They tend to be more rigid, less open-minded, more inflexible, and narrowly conventional. They've lost the capacity to be childlike, and instead of confronting painful problems they escape further into their addiction.

I realize that it is dangerous to generalize at this point, but I find it quite provocative to see that substance and process addictions attract *opposite personality types* in many cases. The difference may be largely due to the fact that process addictions don't carry the same heavy weight of societal disapproval that substance addictions do. (Someone who is very conventional, for example, is not likely to try illegal drugs in the first place.) Other factors may be at work as well.

What this means is that while no particular personality type may be linked with any particular addiction, personality may well help determine whether an individual develops a substance addiction or a process addiction. As I have stated, all addicts share the need to escape the reality of life's difficulties. But whether a person takes the low road of alcohol or drugs or the more subtle pathway of overwork, obsessive involvement in religious activities, or compulsive gambling may well depend on that person's personality. Nonconventionality may predispose one person to try drugs; rigidity or conventionality may turn another toward hidden addictions.

2. A further startling revelation I have gained from my own observation of the personalities of substance and process addicts is *just how pervasive and powerful the many motives for both types of addiction are.*

In the previous section I described how a substance addiction may start with one motive and then move to a second, third, or more motives. These changes help to build psychological dependence. The tree of addiction puts down many roots to sustain its growth. Each root is a "reason" for the addiction that gives pleasure or avoids pain. Cutting down such a tree is very difficult. When you think you've cut off one root and shut off that motive, you discover that there is another and another sustaining the addiction.

Behavior addictions *also* have many roots sustaining them. The tree of workaholism, for example, may begin with one root—say, the desire to make money. But as the overwork continues and the money rolls in, the addict discovers other sources of pleasure in work. The need for power or to prove something to a deceased parent or the search for self-fulfillment may all become major factors in sustaining the addiction. A hidden addiction, therefore, may well be sustained by many underlying motivations. There may be one original or "tap" root, but others can be just as effective in keeping it in place. If psychological factors make substance addictions difficult to eradicate, they make hidden addictions even harder to uproot.

PERSONALITY TYPES IN HIDDEN ADDICTIONS

As I have shown, the idea that any one "personality type" is linked to any particular substance addiction cannot be proved—there is no "alcoholic personality," for instance. The same is true for process addictions; no direct link between a specific personality and a particular hidden addiction can be determined. When it comes to *general* personality traits, however, we can see more of a link, although once again we have to be careful to separate *addicting traits* from *addictive traits*. Characteristics such as high conformity and reward seeking are often seen both before and after a problem with addiction develops, whereas low self-esteem and negative thinking often develop only after a problem has set in.

There are many ways we can approach our identification of "types" of hidden addicts. The approach I have taken is to characterize them by their underlying motivations. People take up different behaviors for different reasons and incorporate them into their lives. The following suggested grouping of process addicts—based on my own clinical experience—is therefore based on the underlying purposes served by the addiction.

1. *Self-Seeking.* These people are similar in make-up to problem drinkers. They have personal problems and anxieties. They tend to ruminate a lot, have difficulty concentrating, and generally lack persistence. They are often shy and don't find it easy to relate to other people.

Their motivation is to *search for some activity or behavior that will relieve their anxiety.* The activity serves as a tranquilizer; it calms them.

Examples of these hidden addictions include addictions to worry, to helping needy people, to social isolation and withdrawal, and to pouting.

2. *Thrill Seeking.* These people are driven by an excessive

need for excitement and stimulation. They are given to curiosity about "new" experiences, are carefree, irrational, extroverted, and usually emotionally immature. Whenever they are unable to find the stimulation they crave, they become moody and feel down.

Thrill seekers are motivated to *experience excitement and escape monotony.* Examples of these hidden addictions include risk-taking, thrill-seeking, sex, and excessive game playing. They become oriented to food, drink, activity, and other pleasure-giving experiences. They are also at high risk for experimenting with drugs.

TABLE 2
Are You a Thrill Seeker?

Read each of the following statements clearly, then check whether it is mostly TRUE or FALSE for you.

TRUE FALSE

____ ____ 1. I often wish I had lived in the unsettled and challenging days of history.

____ ____ 2. I like lots of variation in my life and get depressed when things are dull and boring.

____ ____ 3. High-speed chases in movies or on TV are exciting for me.

____ ____ 4. I read magazines about such dangerous sports as parachuting, motorcycling, or scuba diving.

____ ____ 5. Even though I am not a gambler, I do enjoy the thought of betting on some game or event because I like to predict the outcome.

____ ____ 6. Whenever a crisis arises, I come alive and invariably take charge of the situation.

____ ____ 7. I have never been afraid of heights, snakes, or darkness, even as a small child.

TRUE FALSE

___ ___ 8. Whenever I take a swim, I prefer to jump right into the ocean or cold pool than to enter it slowly.

___ ___ 9. Physical pain doesn't really bother me much.

___ ___ 10. I enjoy real-life drama on TV and seeing policemen actually carrying out a raid.

___ ___ 11. I am not afraid of seeing a dead body; in fact, I find the idea somewhat intriguing.

___ ___ 12. I enjoy teasing others by leaning over the edge of a high balcony or balancing a valuable object in my hand.

___ ___ 13. I often fantasize that I am performing some heroic or exhilarating act, or doing something greatly admired by others.

___ ___ 14. If someone challenges me to do something risky, I have a strong urge to respond.

___ ___ 15. I don't have much respect for people who are cautious or who never enjoy excitement or challenge.

___ Total Number of TRUE responses

Scoring: Total up the number of TRUE responses and use the following table for interpretation:

0 to 3   You have an average amount of thrill seeking.

4 to 8   Your thrill seeking tendencies are moderate to significant.

9 to 12 Your thrill seeking tendencies are quite severe— a major part of your personality.

13 to 15 Thrill seeking dominates your life. You may need help in bringing it under control.

Thrill seeking is a very powerful motivator of addiction. Because it affects so many in our society, I've provided a short test (table 2) to help you identify whether you have this particular personality trait. If you score high on the test, you are at particular risk for developing an addiction.

3. *Self-Deficient.* These people suffer from low or diminished self-esteem long before they develop an addiction. They feel the need to "prove" to themselves or others that they are worthy. They often indulge in fantasy about becoming a big star, achieving monetary success, or accomplishing heroic deeds.

Such people are searching for *self-mastery to prove their self-worth.* They need a boost to overcome deep-seated feelings of insecurity.

People with this personality type may develop addictions to sexual activity (in which sexual prowess is sought to prove self-worth), sporting activities (either actual participation or vicarious involvement—the "armchair jock"), and forms of workaholism.

4. *High-Conforming.* These people "follow the crowd"; they do whatever others do. In fact, the addictions they develop are often addictions to *copying others* as much as to the actual subject of the addiction. These addicts are very group dependent. They must be with people, and they feel miserable when alone. They need the assurance of others and lack self-direction or the ability to affirm their own actions.

They are *searching for company to stabilize their insecurities.* Examples of this kind of hidden addictions include addictions to group activities and to certain other people.

5. *Socially Isolated.* These people are loners. When they jog, they insist on doing it alone. When they work, they do it alone. They don't want the responsibilities of relationships. They prefer to have no permanent contacts. They are unsure of themselves and avoid getting too close to other people for fear of being known for what they really are. They fear

themselves, so they avoid people who might force them to confront their true selves. They avoid intimacy except with a very few long-term friends (usually going back to childhood).

These addicts are *searching for comfort in their isolation.* The hidden addictions such a person develops include addictions to TV watching, collecting unusual objects, solitude, and similar solitary activities.

6. *Self-Punishing.* These people derive pleasure from pain. They are often racked by neurotic guilt and an overwhelming sense of their own inadequacies and failures. They often engage in self-hurtful behaviors, but are not aware that they do this. They use depression as a form of self-punishment and don't allow themselves to enjoy pleasure.

People like this are *searching for pain to resolve neurotic guilt.* The hidden addictions they develop involve behaviors that are self-hurting and destroy contentedness, such as the excessive use of sarcasm or other ways of hurting the very people they desire to love, and excessive devotion to duty (one of the many forms of workaholism). I have often seen this latter addiction in pastors who work excessively despite receiving little reward for their labor and who cannot tolerate any recreation. Such excessive devotion to duty is invariably a way of assuaging a supersensitive conscience. Addictions to rage and resentment would also fall into this category.

It is often not possible to identify a distinct type of personality behind every hidden addiction, of course. As in drug and alcohol addiction, between eight and ten percent indulge their addictions for no identifiable reason, and many more display combinations of the above personality types. For example, a workaholic may be both "self-deficient" and a "self-punisher." He or she may feel very inadequate and also be caught in the clutches of an oversensitive conscience. For such a person, the overwork is an attempt to earn self-respect and praise and also to appease a rigid and inflexible conscience. (Our society tends to reinforce addicts like this. Business and industry thrive on "work junkies." But families and the addicts themselves pay the penalty.)

Not only can mixed personality types give rise to a particular form of hidden addiction; a given personality configuration can also cause several addictions in the same person. For instance, a person with low self-esteem ("self-deficient") and excessive dependency may be prone to excessive work *and* to addictive forms of depression. Mixed process and substance addictions can also arise, as when a workaholic who cannot sleep becomes addicted to the sleeping pills or alcohol he or she ingested to bring on drowsiness.

CONCLUSION

This overview of how personality factors contribute to problems of addiction shows clearly that the relationship is complex. Some traits probably predispose us to certain addictions, while the same traits can lead to more than one kind of dependency. To understand one person's addiction tendencies, we must look not only at his or her *personality*, but also at his or her *environment* or life situation and *unique set of needs*.

It is a mistake to assume that an addiction is less serious or easier to overcome just because it is "hidden" and in the realm of behavior rather than external substances. Remember, psychological dependence—not physical dependence— is the major problem in substance addictions. Therefore, process addictions, which also involve psychological dependence (and may involve physical dependence as well) can be just as devastating and even more resistant to change.

I am firmly convinced that the pain of the mind is worse than the pain of the body. Any person who has suffered from a mental disorder will tell you this. It is also easier to control the body's activities than it is the mind's. If it were not that I believed we have spiritual resources for dealing with the mind, I would give up being a psychotherapist. But God has not left us destitute. As we continue our exploration, the priority of spiritual resources for healing will become more obvious and hopeful.

FOUR

The Addictive Cycle

WHILE OUR GOVERNMENT AND SOCIETY in general have declared all-out war on illegal drugs, many insist that it is a battle that can never be won—because in essence it is a war against human nature. In other words, the pursuit of happiness through chemicals—whether cocaine, caffeine, or biochemicals in the brain—is a universal and inescapable fact of life. Human existence is so precarious and fraught with tension-producing hazards that the desire to alter one's state of consciousness has become almost as basic a drive as hunger and thirst. In fact, these basic drives are often recruited to participate in the masking and tranquilizing of human pain.

Sara understands this well. She experiences her addiction almost daily. Her drug? Food! And not just ordinary food. Sara craves high energy foods—ice cream, nuts, and chocolate—because they are the only ones that can make her feel better. At age twenty-eight she is at least forty pounds overweight and has given up any attempt to reduce. In trying every imaginable diet, she discovered that her anxiety level became intolerable when she deprived herself of her edible "fix."

Sara's problem started when she was a teenager. The photographs she showed me of herself at age thirteen showed a slender, athletic girl. Then, when she was about fourteen, tensions escalated in her parents' relationship that finally led to their divorce. Sara felt sad, lonely, and depressed, and she began reaching for cookies or candy bars to help her cope.

An only child, Sara had no one to talk to about her problems and feelings, so tranquilizing her feelings with a high dose of fats and carbohydrates became a habit. Food made her mellow; it soothed her tangled nerves. And as the years rolled by her dependence on food intensified to the point that she experienced intense anxiety just at the thought of not having food close at hand. Whenever she traveled she stuffed candy into the pockets of her carry-on bag. Her desk at work was a virtual candy store. Almost every room in her condominium had its secret cache of snacks. She had a tangible fear of being caught in an earthquake and not being able to get to the supermarket for several days.

I have worked in therapy with many agoraphobics— people who are literally imprisoned in their homes by anxiety—but I can truthfully say that Sara's addiction was as much a prison as any agoraphobic's home. She was trapped by her need for food—totally obsessed with how to store it, retrieve it, and have it readily available.

Fortunately, Sara was highly motivated and a quick learner. Today, after several years of treatment, she is enjoying a happier and slimmer life. However, treating her addiction involved much more than helping her lose weight. Treating an addiction like Sara's involves coming to under- stand the fundamental drives that led to the addiction in the first place and that continue to maintain it.

It is important to realize that simply forcing an addict to stop an addictive behavior rarely works in the long term. Since the function of an addiction is to place a buffer between ourselves and our awareness of feelings, wrench- ing the buffer away results in increased anxiety. The original addiction is likely to return full force—or be replaced by another one.

A much more effective beginning to overcoming an addiction is to understand how the cycle of addiction works—the many steps and changes that take place as an addiction develops and the addictive behavior is repeated. The better that addicts understand why they behave as they do, the more effective their attempts to change will be.

In Sara's case, she had to come to understand how and why she ran away from emotional pain. She had to learn how to recognize her pain, confront it openly, talk about it, then exercise her choices in a responsible way. Previously she had become so preoccupied with the addiction itself—the food and how to keep its supply lines open—that she had given no thought to the underlying processes of initiation and maintenance.

Although each individual addiction has its own unique process of initiation and maintenance, two basic drives or fundamental needs can be behind all addictions: excitement seeking and tension reducing. In other words, while all addictions generally have to do with pleasure, this pleasure can be the result of excitement (stimulation) or tension reducing. These two drives are directly related to the two basic categories of drugs (stimulants and tranquilizers) discussed in chapter 2. They are so essential to the addiction process that I cannot think of any addiction (substance or hidden) that does not proceed by means of one or the other of these functions—or by a combination of both.

Excitement seeking and tension reducing are basically psychological functions. Even though there may be underlying internal chemical changes that go along with these functions (they may play a significant role even in non-chemical addictions), the cycle of addiction takes place primarily in the mind. This does not mean that it is less powerful than physical processes. As I have said before: the pain of the mind is far worse than the pain of the body.

The addictive need, begun and perpetuated through excitement seeking and tension reducing, is fed constantly in our culture. Clicking your way through all ninety-nine channels of a typical cable TV network ought to convince you of both the pervasive need for these two functions and the extent to which culture supports their fulfillment. (I will confess that on several occasions, usually when I'm tired and bored, I have clicked the remote controls all the way through over and over again, without pausing for more than five or ten seconds on any one of them. Doing that doesn't give you much exercise, but it sure gives you a quick tour of where our culture is headed.)

Unfortunately, the evangelical subculture of which I am a part is no exception to this general observation. As I compare what I see on Christian television with some of what I see on secular TV, for instance, I sometimes have difficulty telling which is which. The music is beginning to sound the same; the flashy clothes and program titles are equally spectacular. And both offer quick fixes for those seeking excitement or a reduction of tension.

Please understand. I believe Christian television can be a wonderful means of grace—bringing the message of God's love right into the home with an impact unknown in previous eras. But it can also make the "wealth and success" gospel (designed to excite or reduce tension) an intimate temptation and create desires that can easily grow into addictions without some balancing influence. More and more Christians are being driven to believe that success is their birthright and that God promises all who follow him a "flower-strewn pathway" free of all pain and problems. Such a Christianity is doomed to failure—as well as being unbiblical. The Christ of the Gospels never promised that sort of nirvana.

Contrary to what our culture tells us, we are not made for constant excitement, and tension cannot (nor should it) always be reduced. Continued excitement quickly becomes no excitement, and a tension-free life is not the happiest. Real satisfaction comes only from balanced living—not from escaping life.

EXCITEMENT SEEKING AND THE ADDICTIVE PROCESS

To experience excitement as one form of pleasure is one of the fundamental abilities given to living beings. And our greatest capacity to enjoy excitement is given to us humans through the marvelous organ we call the brain. In fact, the desire for the pleasure of excitement is such a basic part of normal behavior that the lack of this desire is considered pathological. We call such a person "anhedonic"—unable to experience joy or pleasure.

Some of the most potent drug addictions are based on excitement seeking. One of the reasons why cocaine is so addictive is that it stimulates the pleasure/excitement centers of the brain. For this reason, it is often used as an aid to seduction and an enhancer of sexual excitement. The same is true of "ecstasy," a relatively new drug that was once used in psychotherapy but "hit the street" in the mid-1980s.

But obviously, drug dependencies are not the only kind of excitement-based addiction; many hidden addictions have their counterparts also. The voyeur, the hearty eater, the scientist trying to prove her hypothesis, the cliff climber, the body-building athlete, and the power-wielding boss may all have one thing in common: their behavior provides them with excitement. Our marvelous brain, given by God with the capacity to experience pleasure and excitement, can convert almost any behavior into enjoyment for enjoyment's sake—hence our appetite for addictions.

EXCITEMENT HAS ITS PRICE

Excitement plays an important role in human life; it adds a vital quality to life. Some degree of stimulation, therefore, is desirable; it has a firm basis in how we are designed. Our biology depends on periodic arousal to enhance natural tranquilizers and, as we are now discovering, to recruit disease-fighting cells. Our immune systems function best when we are happiest.

But here comes the rub: *Human beings are not designed for continuous excitement.* Permanent stimulation is no pleasure at all; to maintain the feeling of pleasure, the amount or frequency of the provocative substance or activity must continually be raised. It's like taking a hot bath. The comfort of the warmth soon passes off as the body gets used to it. So to continue feeling warm you must add more hot water—and the body just adapts to the warmer water again. I've added hot water until I was ready to be poached and my body still kept adjusting to the heat. There's a limit, of course, but you could easily reach dangerous levels of heat this way—and still keep crying for more!

What then is the price of excitement? Simple: You can never get enough of it.

Stimulation is only pleasure when it is felt against a background of non-excitement; it can never remain a permanent state. This is where many addicts (substance or process) are led astray. They become driven by a need to maintain constant gratification. They are searching for perpetual arousal. And because they don't understand how pleasure works, they are trapped by their ongoing and ultimately fruitless quest.

What, then, should we know about excitement's pitfalls, and how can we break the addiction process that our search for stimulation maintains? Here are some suggestions:

1. *Begin by reordering your spiritual values and beliefs about the root of pleasure.* Proverbs 21:17 tells us that "he that loveth

pleasure shall be a poor man." Jesus also warned us that the "riches and pleasure of this life" are thorns that choke the Word (Lk 8:14). These are not idle warnings. They come to us from the God who created us and therefore knows us better than we will ever know ourselves. Pleasure seeking through excitement or stimulation, when it is excessive or persistent, and perhaps even long before this, is a product of moral and spiritual poverty. Behind the contemporary facades of wealth, success, power, and popularity is a spiritual ghetto where men and women search for instant and constant intoxication through sex, drugs, and other destructive practices. But let's not be so smug about it. Behind the doors of our Christian homes and in many pews of our places of worship, the same drive for constant spiritual stimulation and the equivalents of wealth, success, signs, and power can just as easily entrap us.

2. *Accept that a "deficit in excitement" is as normal as being overcome by pleasure.* Work and play, excitement and apathy, euphoria and pain—these are points and counterpoints of a healthy life. They are like valleys and hills—the one is necessary for the other to be seen.

I grew up in the Transvaal of southern Africa. This entire region is a large escarpment or plain more than a mile above sea level. This is higher than most mountains. Yet as a child growing up I saw no real mountains. All during my childhood, I was standing on a mountaintop and didn't know it. I needed valleys to show me how high I was.

We need our times of boredom and even sadness to make meaning out of our happiness. The one cannot exist without the other. Unless you have valleys, you don't have mountains. And unless there are times of low arousal or grinding routine, you cannot enjoy a weekend off. Anyone who has recently retired will tell you that having all the time in the world to relax does not bring relaxation.

Our inability to tolerate any deficit in stimulation is a major force in creating addictions. It is especially a major factor in maintaining workaholism, as I know to my detriment. I used to suffer from a feeling of letdown after working hard. For instance, if I spoke at a weekend seminar in some church or conference, I hated being taken back to the airport to catch my plane because waiting for the flight home always set me up for a downer.

I now know this feeling as "postadrenaline depression" because it comes from the switching off of an overused adrenal system. Before I knew this and how important it was to healing, I would try to keep my adrenaline up. I would read, talk to people, take a walk—anything to keep my adrenaline pumping and avoid the letdown.

Then I realized I was just delaying the inevitable. My downers came because my system was craving rest—so why not give it what it needs? By changing my attitude and accepting that I needed to rest, I discovered a wonderful bonus: I have actually come to enjoy the down feeling that comes over me when I have been overstressed. It is my friend, my ally; it aids my healing and it slows me down so I can keep up with God. The "downtime" following periods of hard work is a "pleasure-deficit" period (a valley if you prefer) that gives value and enjoyment to my pleasure peaks.

I now thank God for my low periods, and doing this has reduced my need to be doing something constantly. I commend this change in attitude to you also.

3. *Watch where and how you get your excitement.* My emphasis on the dangers of excitement seeking should not be taken to mean that we should avoid pleasure. As I have indicated, pleasure and stimulation have their place. The important questions are *where* we seek excitement and *how* we seek it.

The *where* question is the biggie. Alcohol, sex, gambling, pornography—the list of the obviously harmful sources of stimulation is long. In the area of hidden addictions however, *where* has more to do with neurotic needs and doing things to excess. We have to guard against the needs that may arise out of low self-esteem, a search for love or respect, or a need to be powerful. In their own way, these "places" are as deadly as any "crack" house or bar.

How you get your stimulation is also important. Running away from boredom or isolation, bombarding yourself with stimuli (for instance, always needing a radio or TV to be on) or becoming excessively competitive can all predispose us to hidden addictions.

4. *Come to appreciate "satisfaction" over "excitement."* Pleasure means different things to different people, so I don't want to seem pedantic here. However, I think there is a world of difference between "satisfaction" and "stimulation."

If unremitting excitement is no pleasure, then I would say that satisfaction is the exact opposite: there is *no* limit to the amount of satisfaction you can experience. You can never become addicted to real peace!

Perhaps you've never thought about this distinction before. But substituting the pursuit of satisfaction for the pursuit of excitement can revolutionize your life.

How do I distinguish between excitement and satisfaction? I see excitement as a feeling—of enjoyment, delight, and gratification of the senses. Satisfaction is more basic. It has a strong element of contentment. It also brings pleasure. But rather than being the presence of a strong positive emotion, it is the absence of a negative one. It is a "resting" from one's labors.

Satisfaction also has an other-directed quality; it results from seeking to give rather than seeking to receive. Whereas the general direction of pleasure is always *toward* the self, the general direction of satisfaction is always *away* from the self. When I *receive* a gift, for example, the direction is toward me and I derive *excitement*. When I *give* a gift, the direction is *away* from me, and I derive *satisfaction*. I can become satiated by receiving too many gifts because excitement can be overloaded. Mostly, I can never give too many gifts! Of course, if you are not careful even giving can be stimulating and it is then possible to become addicted to it. However, this behavior is uncommon, and I wouldn't be too concerned about it.

True satisfaction, then, never builds an addiction. There are no excitement centers being stimulated; there are no neurotic needs to be met. When a job is well done or I keep a promise, I feel deep satisfaction. When I help a needy person or fulfill a responsibility, I feel indescribable satisfaction. The direction is always away from me, but the benefit is deep within my being. Satisfaction never leaves a compelling hunger for more. Excitement always does!

Focusing on being more outwardly directed and less preoccupied with ourselves and our own needs is an effective antidote for any addiction because it breeds satisfaction, and satisfaction breeds contentment, and, as the Epistle of Timothy tells us, contentment with godliness is great gain. (See 1 Timothy 6:6.)

The whole theme of *contentment* is a fascinating one to me as a Christian psychologist. It surprises me how little credit it is given in secular psychology and how seldom it figures in most systems of psychotherapy. To avoid creating an addiction, however, it is vital. And it doesn't take ten years of therapy to create it. In fact, Scripture presents it as a simple act of the will: "And having food and raiment let us be therewith content" (1 Tm 6:8).

That's it: simply "be content." Choose it over discontent, which is destructive to the body, mind, and spirit and is the foundation stone for addiction. If you suffer from more than your fair share of discontent, I strongly prescribe some time spent in prayer, asking God to help you turn your attitude around. Unless you can do this, you will always be at risk for addiction.

Proverbs 30:15-16 captures the addiction dilemma well. These verses tell us that there are four things in this world that are never satisfied: hell, barrenness, drought, and fire. In many respects an addiction feels like these terrible things. It is a hell and a drought—and nothing can satisfy it. The same is true with discontentment.

TENSION REDUCTION AND THE ADDICTIVE PROCESS

Remember, excitement seeking is only one side of the addictive process. The other is *tension reduction*. Many addictions are created and maintained because the addictive behavior helps reduce tension in the addict's life.

Like excitement seeking, tension reduction meets some real needs and has its positive side. Relaxation and recreation should be a part of a balanced life. But they must come *after* problems have been engaged and solved. They should never be a means of escaping pain—as they become in tension-reducing addictive behavior.

Bob, for instance, is a well-to-do attorney with a hectic schedule and a chaotic work style. As a consequence, he drives his secretary up the wall. He is always late in giving her briefs to type and therefore she often has to work through the night to get material ready for him the next day. Then she threatens to resign, and he has to plead with her and promises to change his ways. But in the ten years she has worked for Bob, nothing has ever changed. Bob is just a disorganized person.

But Bob pays for this disorganization. He goes home at night exhausted and confused. His neck hurts and his head aches. He often has diarrhea, and the doctor has warned him that his cholesterol is sky-high. Bob recalls that his father, who had also been an attorney before his fatal heart attack at age fifty-seven, was the same way. In fact, it frightens him to look in the mirror sometimes, because at thirty-seven he thinks he sees his father in the reflection.

Early in his practice as an attorney, Bob discovered that if he preoccupied himself with his coin collection he could reduce his tension and regather his calm, so he began spending every spare moment with his coins. Oh, he was careful at first to give his wife and little daughter some of his time. He played with them, joked with them, and even listened to what they had to say, but all the time his eye was on the clock. As his daughter's bedtime drew near, his anticipation intensified. Then he would dash to the corner of the family room where he kept his collection. For several hours he would examine, touch, explore, and catalog his collection. And as he "played" with them his tension dissolved, his conflicts resolved themselves, and even his depressions were relieved. He felt secure with his coins. They were valuable—and he dreamed that one day they might even make him rich.

Bob never showed his coins to others. They were a private part of him. The more pressure during the day, the more he needed his passionate hobby to reduce that tension. Unlike a normal hobby that provides distraction and a degree of pleasure, his dependence on a "process" of coin jingling became excessive and began to serve many functions deep within his psyche. It was his sole coping mechanism and his only source of comfort. It helped him to escape the realities of his life. It finally became a true addiction.

Bob's wife became frustrated with his preoccupation and didn't know how to help him. Fortunately, she finally had the courage to declare, "Enough is enough! Get help or I'm leaving you." Bob sought help, and eventually came to understand how his addiction served to reduce his tensions.

There is a large body of research literature that explores the relationship between unendurable life circumstances and the development of addiction. Many researchers single out unpleasant emotional tensions as the cause of the addictive process in these cases. Such emotions include anxiety, depression, hostility, shame, guilt, feelings of inferiority, disappointment, boredom, panic, fear, and loneliness. Some experts even believe that a disturbed capacity to cope with positive emotions—love, tenderness, intimacy, or friendliness—is a root cause in many addictions. The addictive behavior serves to relieve the inner tension brought on by these emotions, just as excitement can provide a way to escape the reality of these unpleasant feelings.

HOW ADDICTIONS REDUCE TENSION

Some addictions fulfill the function of reducing tension through four sequential steps:

1. *The addict experiences an unmet need or painful life situation.* Boredom, conflict with friends or family, a crisis, pain, or any of the negative emotions mentioned above creates tension or stress. Many different factors may come into play at this point. Constitutional or genetic factors will affect how much stress you can take before negative emotions develop. Modeling from parents and peers will also play a part in determining how you react to certain situations or emotions. Your social milieu will then expose you to possibly addictive behaviors and reinforce your attraction to them. Family factors such as overindulgence, chaos, or conflict can create excessive and distorted needs. A daughter, for example, who does not get adequate love from a father may well spend the rest of her life searching for this missing love in many disruptive male relationships. But since none of these is capable of being her father, her search is doomed to frustration. She becomes addicted to her search for love.

2. *The unmet need creates a "pressure" or imbalance that can only be relieved by engaging in some behavior.* The "surrender" to this behavior thus becomes the addiction.

3. *With the "surrender" to the behavior comes a sense of relief, then denial.* The relief in some cases may be profound. With it comes a reduction in need and a denial that the behavior that was engaged in had anything to do with the relief.

Denial plays a formative role in all addictions. In fact, it seems that for a behavior to become addicting, the relief it provides must be denied. The more unconscious the connection between the need and the behavior that brings relief, the more powerful the addiction. It's as if the mind conspires to keep the addiction "game" secret. Somehow this helps to make the behavior more effective as a tension reducer.

Notice that I am not just saying that the addicted person denies that he or she engages in some addictive behavior. I'm saying more than this. The addict denies that the behavior relieves tension—that it serves any purpose whatsoever. A great degree of rationalization then takes place. "I collect coins because it's a good investment." "I gamble because buying lottery tickets benefits our schools and the next generation of kids." "I work hard because my kids deserve a better start in life than I got." One could write a book about these "excuses" for addiction.

The connection between denial and the drive to engage in the addictive behavior is so strong that the very presence of denial, and any subsequent rationalization, can be taken as strong evidence that an addiction is present.

4. *Once the addictive behavior is completed, the tension reappears.* The tension relief that occurs in addictions, like the pleasure they afford, is temporary and ultimately unsatisfactory. Sooner or later the tension reemerges and the unbearable life circumstance surfaces again. This recreates a need for the behavior, and the cycle begins again.

TRIGGER MECHANISMS FOR ADDICTIVE BEHAVIOR

The two major drives that underlie the addictive process, excitement seeking and tension reduction, are often "set off" by a particular starting stimulus. We can call this the "trigger mechanism" for the addiction. It is the emotion or occurrence that starts a given cycle of addictive behavior.

Let's imagine that Dave, a fictitious salesman, is generally bored with his job, but he loves to ski. Skiing is the only source of real excitement in Dave's life; he lives for the snow slopes and dreams about nothing else. Clearly he is an addict because he neglects every other aspect of his life.

Now, say it is Friday morning. Dave usually spends Fridays in the office writing up orders and processing his paperwork. This is a part of his job he particularly hates. Every form, letter, or purchase order is like poison to him; he even dislikes touching them.

Dave checks his watch. Nine-thirty in the morning. Still six and a half hours to go before quitting time. He tries to concentrate, but the dull routine of his job acts as a stimulus for his addictive need. Boredom is the trigger for his addiction craving. He wants to be on the mountain. He wants to feel the cold chill of the wind and hear the swoosh of the skis. He checks his watch again. Only 9:50. The more bored Dave becomes, the more he craves his skiing fix. It's going to be a long day!

Trigger mechanisms like Dave's boredom begin the addictive craving for a given cycle of need. They differ from person to person and from addictive behavior to addictive behavior. Often the roots of these trigger mechanisms can be traced to experiences we disliked as a child. Here are some common triggers:

- anxiety,
- isolation,
- boredom,
- depression,
- crises,
- sense of failure,
- unmet sexual needs,
- criticism,
- selfish needs.

The last of the above list, selfish needs, is a major trigger for many addictions. Technically known as "polarized narcissism," it is usually found in people who have suffered from early life disruption or damage and whose nurturance and dependency needs have not been met. Such people often develop a deep desire for instant gratification. They know where, when, and how they want it—and they want it now! For instance, they demand instant and excessive affirmation for even small attempts at work or in relationships. The needs of others never enter the picture. They are focused only on their own needs.

There are many other possible triggers for addictive behavior. In fact, *anything that threatens failure*, rejection, or abandonment can become a stimulus for an addiction cycle. Add to this the personality traits of passivity, under-assertiveness, or dependency, and you have a powerful set of addictive triggers.

INTERRUPTING THE CYCLE OF NEED

How can an addictive process be broken once it has begun? As I have indicated in early chapters, this is not easy—but it is possible. Here are some suggestions:

1. *The addict should try to identify whether the addiction is maintained by the drive of excitement seeking, tension reduction, or both.* The greater his or her understanding of the dynamics of the addiction, the greater his or her ability to overcome it.

2. *Addicts that are predominantly excitement seekers should concentrate on being content with the "ordinary" and developing an appetite for "satisfaction" rather than stimulation.* Thrill-seeking addicts need to learn how to be content with "ordinary" activities and increase their appreciation for the "little" joys of life. Overstimulation creates satiation. Therefore, overcoming an excitement-seeking addiction involves learning how to live with less arousal and allowing your body and

mind to become accustomed to lowered arousal.

3. *Tension reducers need to focus on identifying their painful emotions more accurately and understanding how these emotions lead to the addictive behaviors.* The goal here is to teach oneself how to confront pain head-on, with full engagement of reality. In addition, because denial is such a powerful force, addicts need to increase their awareness of their denial tendencies, undoing their tendency to misinterpret, confuse the issue, or split off their feelings from reality. Ask a close friend or spouse to give honest feedback, for instance. Or build a small support group of trusted friends with whom you can share your tensions.

4. *Addicts should pay attention to the trigger mechanisms that serve as stimulants to an addictive cycle.* Knowing the kind of circumstances that tend to "kick off" addictive behavior means that the addict can either avoid the trigger or formulate a plan for keeping the trigger from "working."

5. *Addicts need to find alternative ways of responding to their trigger mechanisms.* This means learning to deal with need in a more wholesome way. For instance, if boredom is a trigger, the addict needs to learn some way of handling boredom without resorting to the addictive behavior. If the trigger is depression, the addict must seek help in discovering the underlying *cause* of the depression and overcoming it. Suppressing depression never cures it—it only prolongs the depression.

6. *Parents need to recognize how to avoid raising addiction-prone children.* We know that children of alcoholics have become alcoholics—partly because they were raised with their parents modeling addictive behavior to them. The same is true for the children of workaholics, shopaholics, compulsive gamblers, and other process addicts. Children learn what they see, and therefore many hidden addictions are passed on from generation to generation with little thought to how this cycle might be stopped.

Because most addictions arise out of the pleasure/pain

axis of life (giving rise to either excitement-seeking or tension-reducing addictions), parents can play a key role in shaping a healthy approach to life. Teaching children how not to be so stimulation- or excitement-bound is not difficult. All it takes is a little forethought, some patience— and a *lot* of personal example. Providing a stable, loving, nurturing, forgiving, and affirming home environment, with plenty of evidence of God's presence in the life of the parents, will be the best guarantee of a balanced life any parent can give a child.

7. *Last, addicts must seek spiritual and psychological healing.* An addiction is a very complex learned response involving the whole person—mind, body, and spirit. The longer one has been controlled by it, the deeper it is entrenched. Lots of hard work is needed to undo these complex connections of thought, nerve, and hormone. I believe that God's intervention is needed as well—whether he works through a direct miracle (I have seen this happen) or through a more natural healing process.

As we proceed to explore specific kinds of hidden addictions, I will attempt to give definitive help both from a spiritual and psychological point of reference. Let me assure you that God *is* interested in your problem and that turning to him *will* empower you for healing. From my experience in working with many hidden addictions I know that God honors our willingness to participate with him in our healing. He doesn't seem to help those who don't seek help; he is wise enough to know how pointless that will be. But to the one who desires it and earnestly seeks God's healing participation, he promises, ". . . All joy and peace in believing, that ye may abound in hope, through the power of the Holy Ghost" (Rom 15:13).

FIVE

Obsessions and Compulsions

N O UNDERSTANDING OF ADDICTIONS in general and hidden
addictions in particular would be complete without an
understanding of how obsessions and compulsions relate to
the addictive process. As I have indicated, many addictions
can have their roots in or involve obsessional thoughts or
compulsive behaviors. At the same time, there is little
connection between addictions and the neurotic afflictions
technically called obsessive or compulsive *disorders or both.*
While there are certain surface similarities, they differ
significantly in cause, mechanism, and treatment. In this
chapter I will try to outline both the differences between the
two and points at which they are related.

OBSESSIONS

Maria is a quiet, somewhat reserved single woman of
thirty-four. She still lives with her elderly parents, who are
somewhat incapacitated and dependent on her. Taking care
of them while holding down a job in the telephone company
leaves her with little time for recreation. Regular church

73

attendance is about all the excitement there is in her life.

About six months ago, Maria began to experience frequent, uncontrollable thoughts. She finds them repugnant, which is why she sought therapy. At times she imagines her parents are dead and she is burying them in a grave. The images are vividly clear. She sees herself first digging the grave, then placing her parents in the hole, then throwing dirt on them. Try as she can, she cannot stop these thoughts. In fact, the more she tries to stop them, the stronger they get.

Maria has begun to fear going to bed at night. She delays as long as possible, staying up until she is so exhausted that she drops off to sleep immediately. She also fears waking up at night because the frightening thoughts overwhelm her—she can't control them.

Maria is experiencing a bout with obsessional thinking—a fairly common anxiety problem that has its origins in the conflict she feels about her parents. She loves them, yet she resents having to put her life on "hold" in order to care for them. (She is their only child, and no one else in the family wants the responsibility.) She fears for her future. Just how long will this situation go on? She really doesn't want them to die. She just wishes she were freer to live her own life. "What if I fall in love with someone? He won't want to be burdened by them. My life is wasted before it has begun."

The obsessional thoughts began when, in a fit of anger, she shouted at her father, "I wish you were dead." She didn't mean it, and she tried to retract her words. She spent several days feeling intense guilt over her actions. Then the intrusive thoughts began. "I mustn't think these thoughts," she told herself, "they are evil." But the more she tried to block them, the stronger they became.

Now, Maria's problem is *not* an addiction. Her obsessional thoughts, like an addiction, are a response to painful feelings, and like an addiction they are difficult to control. But there are distinct differences, as we will see.

We are *all* capable of obsessional thinking—the tendency to fixate on certain thoughts. The great Russian novelist Leo Tolstoy, for instance, once told how his older brother ordered him to "stand in the corner until you stop thinking of a white bear." Poor Leo. It seemed simple enough, but he found himself standing helplessly in the corner, unable to stop thinking about a white bear. This is the dynamic of an obsession. We can be consumed by thoughts we are trying hard to suppress. The harder we try to suppress them the more they devour us.

Most people seem to have at least one troublesome thought that persistently haunts them. It can be the remembrance of the death of a friend or some frightening experience, or it might be the fear of something we think might happen. This is quite normal. All we have to do to create an obsession is to say to ourselves: "I must never think of that." We'll be trapped before we know it. This also gives a clue as to how a neurotic obsession—especially a minor one—can be removed: by giving ourselves permission to think the thought.

I did this with Maria. She did not suffer from a full-blown obsessional disorder—only an obsessional tendency. "Now, I want you to sit there and think about burying your parents. Tell me about your thoughts as they proceed." I kept her at the task for several sessions in a row. I helped her see that *thinking* something isn't the same as doing it. Maria's obsessional preoccupation soon passed off (unlike severe obsessional states), so we were then able to turn our attention to helping her face her fears and change her living patterns in order to gain some freedom. It just so happened that her parents were nowhere near as incapacitated as she believed they were.

A full-blown obsessional disorder is not cured so easily, however. Here, the obsessions are qualitatively more severe, persistent, and resistant. A person, for example, may persistently have thoughts of poisoning her parents. The thoughts become a source of torment and may even be incapacitating to the point that she refuses to visit her parents. It is a maladaptive response to deep-seated anxiety and is very hard to treat. Both the severe form and the minor variations of obsessional tendencies have the following qualities to varying degrees:

- They involve repetitive, uncontrollable thoughts.
- The obsessional thoughts are meaningless or unwelcome.
- The obsession affords no pleasure.
- The obsession always produces a loss of energy and a sense of ambivalence.
- Severe obsessions destroy healthy mental functioning.
- They involve denial of the underlying anxiety, but not of the thoughts themselves.

The last feature is perhaps the most important feature that distinguishes obsessional tendencies from addictions or any other mental disorder. The victim of an obsession is always *aware* of the obsessional thoughts. He or she may try to hide them, but there is no denial that they exist or that they constitute a problem. However, in its place, there is invariably a denial of the basic tension or anxiety underlying the obsessions.

COMPULSIONS

When my oldest grandson, Vincent, was about five years old, I saw an interesting example of a behavior resembling a compulsion—one you don't read much about these days. It was a compulsion to confess.

Under my bed I usually keep a box of candy as a treat for

my grandchildren. They all know where it is. They also know the rules: "One candy bar, per child, per visit, *if* you ask politely for it ahead of time. If you take a bar without asking or take more than one, you forfeit a treat next time you visit."

Seems reasonable to me! Not only is this "game" a way of making it fun to visit, it also teaches trust and honesty.

One day Vincent sidled up to me while I was sitting in my favorite chair, reading.

"Papa." He was timid. "Is it true that we've got two voices inside?"

"What do you mean?" I asked, very intrigued.

"Well, you know, when you don't do something right—like, well, one voice says, 'that's good, 'cause you didn't get caught.' But the other voice says, 'Yeah, but you didn't keep the rules.' "

"Yes," I replied, still tentative because I had no idea what he was leading up to. "Yes, there are two voices like that inside. Does the one voice want to tell me something?"

"Yes, it wants to say it's sorry 'cause last time I was here I took two candy bars. It doesn't make me feel very good!"

He looked straight into my eyes—waiting for a reaction and expecting the worst.

"I'm very happy that you listened to that other voice and told me," I replied. "What should we do about it?"

"Very easy," was his quick reply. "If I don't take a candy today, then we're quits, right?"

"Right," I said.

He smiled in relief. He knew the rules and it felt better when he kept them.

I was very proud of Vincent that day. What he felt was an irresistible *compulsion to confess* that he had done something wrong.

Vincent's compulsion was quite normal. We all experience an urge to confess when we feel guilty. Psychologically and spiritually it seems that we were designed for confession. It cleanses our hearts like nothing else. *True compulsions,* however, go much further. As with obsessions, compulsions can take the form of minor tendencies or full-blown disorders. They share the following characteristics and differ only in severity and degree of incapacitation.

- They are repetitive, unwelcomed, and alien.
- They are meaningless urges, essentially unconnected with or out of proportion to the relief they provide.
- Often they are trivial or ritualistic.
- The actions are performed against one's will.
- The behavior can be silly or terrifying, or somewhere between these extremes.
- Like obsessions, *they give no pleasure.* Their essential function is to provide *relief* from underlying anxiety.

Vic shows evidence of a full-blown compulsive disorder. Whenever he walks to or from his downtown office from the parking structure, he has to walk on pavements that have paving slabs about two feet square. As he walks on these pavements, he feels driven to avoid stepping on any of the joints. This compulsive avoidance of "stepping on cracks" started some years ago when his boss was "riding him." He was under a lot of strain at work—with tension running high. One day, for some reason, he carefully avoided stepping on the joints on the way to his office. Lo and behold, his day seemed to go better. Ever since then, Vic has been trapped by his silly and meaningless compulsion to avoid the cracks. His pattern has become ingrained. He has told no one else but me about it, and then it only came out accidentally.

Very often, compulsions are directed toward future events; their purpose is to cause or prevent something. However, the compulsive behavior is not connected in any way to the event it is designed to produce or prevent.

As with the obsessions, severe obsessions and compulsions (they often occur together) are *not* the stuff of addictions. They are clearly differentiated disorders of the mind. Obsessive and compulsive *tendencies,* however, could readily lead to addictions. Here are the major differences between the severe disorders and addictions:

1. *In obsessive-compulsive disorders, the thoughts or behaviors create pain, not pleasure.* Even though the obsessive thought or compulsive behavior functions to allay anxiety, the sufferer does not enjoy the thought or the behavior.

2. *Obsessive-compulsives do not deny their lack of control,* although, as I have shown, they may deny the underlying anxiety. They are very aware of their pain.

3. *Obsessive-compulsive disorders do not involve dependence on external or internal chemicals.* To our knowledge, obsessive-compulsive disorders are almost entirely neurotic (that is, psychological) in cause and operation.

In an addiction, therefore, the sufferer has a controlling need or desire for a substance, object, action, or behavior because it produces a pleasant psychophysiological reaction—stimulation or relaxation—but denies that control. In an obsessive-compulsive disorder, the victim is driven by underlying anxiety to repeat certain thoughts and behaviors that he knows are out of his control and may be harmful, but that somehow relieve that underlying anxiety.

Many sufferers of compulsions and obsessions also experience phobias, indecision, doubting, and procrastination—all results of acute, underlying anxiety. *Severe* forms of these disorders require skilled professional help. Fortunately, there is medication now available that can relieve the symptoms of severe obsessions, suggesting that the severe forms of this disorder may have a strong underlying biological component, which is not true in the lesser forms that are more psychological.

THE ADDICTIVE OVERLAP WITH OBSESSIONS AND COMPULSIONS

As I have shown, the severer obsessive and compulsive disorders are a separate disorder of mental functioning *not* directly connected with any addiction. However, lesser forms of obsessiveness and compulsiveness (I call them "tendencies") can exist by themselves even in "normal" people and be a cause for addiction. While only one in about two thousand Americans are affected by a serious obsessive-compulsive disorder, one in four is affected by such obsessive or compulsive tendencies. And while there is little connection between addictions and obsessive-compulsive *disorders,* there *is* a close relationship between addictions and obsessive-compulsive *tendencies.*

Confused? You're not alone. There is much misunderstanding about obsessions, compulsions, and addictions in both lay and professional literature. The confusion may well stem from the basic definitions of the words *obsessive* and *compulsive.* In a basic sense, a person who is "obsessive" is simply one who is preoccupied with certain thoughts. Similarly, a "compulsive" is a person who feels driven or compelled to carry out certain behaviors. In this sense, as we will see, an addict can be or become either obsessive, compulsive, or both. In the case of obsessive-compulsive disorders, however, these words have been applied to specific neurotic disorders that are separate from addiction. But that doesn't rob the words of their basic meaning or make their use in describing other behavior inappropriate.

For instance, someone who has a powerful urge to shop may be a "compulsive shopper" but does not have a classic compulsive disorder. "Compulsive shoppers" find pleasure or relaxation in the act of shopping itself. They can't resist a "special offer," and they accumulate things they don't need. The act of buying gives them a "lift" they find stimulating. If this behavior gets out of control, the shopper is likely to develop an addiction. The compulsive behavior will then continue, intensified.

On the other hand, consider a young man who refuses to touch door knobs with his bare hands. He can't go anywhere without planning how he will be able to avoid opening doors. He is obsessed with the idea that germs are on every knob, and compulsively he washes his hands for fear that even the gloves he wears are insufficient protection. He is trapped by his obsessive-compulsive prison. It pains him and he longs to be free of this disabling handicap.

Clearly, this young man has an obsessive-compulsive disorder. It gives him no pleasure—no satisfaction. It is not simply an obsessive-compulsive tendency but a full-blown disturbance of living. It will not grow into an addiction because a true addiction needs to have some pleasure component.

Obsessive and compulsive tendencies (as opposed to obsessive-compulsive disorders) relate to addiction in two ways:

1. *Obsessive and compulsive tendencies may be symptoms of established addictions.* Once an addiction is established, the addict is almost certain (at least at times) to be obsessed with the addictive substance or behavior and to feel a compulsion to ingest the substance or perform the behavior. Jimmy, for example, is addicted to skiing. He loves the thrill of risk, the feeling of mastery, and the physical pleasure it gives him. He lives for skiing, just as a workaholic lives for work or an alcoholic for alcohol. He daydreams about skiing, watches movies about it, and has posters about it all over his apartment. But these are simply obsessive "tendencies" that have grown out of his addiction—not a true clinical obsession. There is no pain in his preoccupation.

The addict may also have *compulsive tendencies.* He feels driven or compelled to repeat the addicted behavior or ingest the substance over and over. Jimmy can never get enough skiing. Without his "fix" he is miserable. Life has no other meaning for him. But his compulsive urge to ski is *not* the same as his addiction, and it is not a clinical compulsion.

2. *Obsessive and compulsive tendencies may predispose a person to addiction, and minor obsessions or compulsions may grow into addictions.* This point is crucial for people-helpers like me to understand. Shopping may start out as a compulsive tendency. It may help to relieve tension or free the person from anxiety. It provides distraction and some pleasure. But after a while it may begin to recruit addictive-forming adrenaline or some other physiological reactions as well as establishing a memory of pleasant experiences. Soon the simple compulsion begins to dominate the victim's life and a true addiction emerges as this victim loses control over the behavior. But even when the control is lost, the pleasure element remains.

OBSESSIVE-COMPULSIVE PERSONALITIES

When the tendency to be obsessive and compulsive is deeply rooted and has been around a long time, we speak of it as a "personality" problem. This simply means that it is such a deep part of you that it shapes your personality and controls your behavior.

Since obsessive or compulsive tendencies can contribute to the development of addiction, it follows that people with obsessive or compulsive personalities will be prone to develop addictions. And the very nature of these personality types makes development of a *hidden* addiction especially likely.

Tables 3 and 4 provide two simple tests of obsessive and compulsive tendencies to help you understand yourself. The degree of obsessiveness or compulsiveness may vary from "normal" all the way to "severe." Remember, however, that having severe obsessive or compulsive tendencies does *not* mean you have an obsessive-compulsive disorder.

These tests don't tell you whether obsessive or compulsive tendencies are part of your basic personality. This depends on how long you have been this way. Sometimes obsessiveness or compulsiveness can be temporary and tied to excessive tension at a particularly pressured time of life; it passes away as soon as the pressures ease. In people with an obsessive or compulsive personality, however, the obsessive or compulsive traits have become ingrained.

The *obsessive* personality has the following traits:

- excessive rigidity and inflexibility,
- extreme conscientiousness,
- "cold perfectionism,"
- preoccupation with detail,
- indecisiveness and preoccupation,
- "stiff" demeanor,
- awkwardness in handling emotions,
- difficulty relaxing,
- tendency to treat hobbies as tasks rather than fun.

The *compulsive* personality has similar traits, but also may include:

- persistence and endurance (usually beyond the point of reasonableness)
- possessiveness,
- limited social contacts,
- superstitious ideas,
- perfectionism and scrupulosity,
- rigid moral standards,
- perfect tidiness,
- seeks the perfect answer for every choice,
- a master at "second-guessing,"
- inability to accept compromises (even small ones),
- tendency to intellectualize.

TABLE 3

Are You Obsessive?

The following test measures your tendency to engage in obsessive thinking. Read each statement carefully and place a check in either the TRUE or FALSE column, depending on whether the statement is *mostly* true or false for you.

TRUE FALSE

___ ___ 1. When I am sitting in church I tend to count objects I see such as lamps, bricks, or people.

___ ___ 2. I have recurring thoughts that I cannot control.

___ ___ 3. I fantasize or visualize images or behaviors that disturb me, but I cannot seem to put them out of my mind.

___ ___ 4. I have difficulty falling asleep at night because my mind is too active and will not let me rest.

___ ___ 5. I have thoughts of violence (like killing or hurting someone).

___ ___ 6. When I shake hands with someone or touch a faucet or doorknob, I worry about whether I have become infected.

___ ___ 7. I am full of doubts and have difficulty making up my mind whether I believe something or not.

___ ___ 8. I worry about whether I have unknowingly done some harm such as hurting someone in an accident or receiving too much change at the store.

TRUE FALSE

___ ___ 9. The more I try to stop thinking something unpleasant, the more it forces itself into my mind.

___ ___ 10. I am often preoccupied with details about a project or something else I must do.

___ ___ 11. I like to keep to a set daily routine and am upset when the routine is changed.

___ ___ 12. I have to turn things over and over again in my mind before deciding what to do.

___ ___ 13. Generally, I have difficulty making up my mind about almost everything.

___ ___ 14. I have many thoughts that are repugnant or senseless, and the more I try to eliminate them, the stronger they become.

___ ___ 15. I often feel as if my mind is an "enemy within," controlling me, rather than me controlling it.

_____ Total number of TRUE responses:

Scoring: Allow one point for each TRUE response. (The maximum you can score is 15.) The higher the number of TRUE responses, the stronger your obsessive tendencies. Your score can be interpreted as follows:

0 to 2: Normal obsessiveness (We all have a bit of it!)

3 to 5: Moderate obsessiveness, but with a tendency to become overly obsessive in times of stress.

6 to 15: Severe obsessiveness. You tend to be controlled by your obsessiveness and may need help in dealing with severe underlying anxiety.

TABLE 3 (*continued*)

Are You Compulsive?

The following test measures your tendency to be compulsive. Read each statement carefully and place a check in either the TRUE or FALSE column, depending on whether the statement is *mostly* true or false for you.

TRUE FALSE

____ ____ 1. Even when I know I've done something correctly (such as locking the door) I have a need to go back and check it.

____ ____ 2. I often do things I do not really want to do because I have a strong urge to do them.

____ ____ 3. I cannot leave a task partly finished, but continue until it is done.

____ ____ 4. I prefer to have a routine and do the same things the same way every time.

____ ____ 5. I have rules I follow whether it is for doing something or going somewhere.

____ ____ 6. I am strongly controlled by the belief that unless I do something (such as touch a doorknob or say an expression) something unpleasant will happen.

____ ____ 7. I do several things that I consider to be meaningless, yet I feel compelled to do them even against my better judgment.

____ ____ 8. When I have completed something or have performed some behavior I have resisted, I feel a great sense of release from tension.

TRUE FALSE

—— —— 9. I have a strong need to be organized, neat, and tidy.

—— —— 10. I am fairly rigid when it comes to keeping to time schedules and planned activity.

—— —— 11. I often have to do things over because I don't think they have been done right (by myself or others).

—— —— 12. I am very careful about how I fold my clothes when I take them off at night.

—— —— 13. I have a place for everything and carefully put everything back in its place.

—— —— 14. I am a detail person and like to pay attention to detail because I feel more comfortable this way.

—— —— 15. Having left something undone makes me feel very uncomfortable and uneasy.

———————— Total TRUE responses

Scoring: Allow one point for each TRUE response. (The maximum you can score is 15.) The higher the number of true responses, the higher is your score of compulsiveness. Your score can be interpreted as follows:

0 to 2: Normal compulsiveness (we all have a bit of it!).

3 to 5: Moderate compulsiveness, but with a tendency to become compulsive in times of stress.

6 to 15: Severe compulsiveness. Your behavior may work against you, and you can probably do with some help in overcoming it.

Within our Christian communities, people with compulsive personality problems tend to be excessively legalistic and punitive; they see themselves as the "protectors of the faith." They like to administer justice, but without love or understanding. When you strip off the veneer of self-imposed righteousness, the basic drive seems to be one of control and domination. They need to be right, and they want to be seen doing the right. Their self-esteem depends on it.

These personality types may give the appearance of cohesion and integration, honesty and openness—but it is only an appearance. They may believe and feel they have nothing to hide and are entirely open and uncomplicated. But the truth is that they are so afraid of being found out that they build, within their personality, high walls and rigid defenses. Denial of their own shortcomings and deepest feelings is deeply entrenched. But although they hide behind a wall of denial, deep down they are paralyzed with fear:

- fear of failure,
- fear of imperfection,
- fear of being unloved,
- fear of being wrong,
- fear of being left out,
- fear of being contaminated,
- fear of being ignored,
- fear of "losing it" (disintegration of personality).

Once again, having an obsessive personality or a compulsive personality is not equivalent to having an addiction. However, the excessive rigidity of people with this personality type and their use of denial as a defense mechanism make them at risk to develop a hidden addiction.

OBSESSIVE-COMPULSIVE ADDICTIONS

The frequency with which I notice these personality traits in Christians alarms me. I've not made up my mind whether we attract these traits or create them. I do think, however, that we in the church ought to do a better job of helping people with severe obsessive-compulsive tendencies to move to a healthier, more spontaneous personality style.

Several years ago I met a prominent Christian leader who epitomized the obsessive-compulsive personality style. He was an evangelist who traveled all around the country leading crusades. It was his personality that caused him to choose this itinerant work. Even though he could be successful in regular ministry, he could never stay too long in any one place. He just had to move on when things got too familiar and people began to see how rigid he was.

This man was almost a textbook case of inflexibility. He was rigid. There was only one way to do something—his way. He was a perfectionist. The choir had to dress a certain way, stand in a certain place, and sing in a certain style. His preaching was hateful; he spewed out venom. His theology bordered on the superstitious. And if you confronted him, he would deny every one of these descriptions. He was totally out of touch with himself. His wife (who traveled with him when family duties permitted) was a nervous wreck because he would never allow her to express any feelings or talk to him about his problems.

Finally, one day, something snapped, and this evangelist took off with a younger woman, never to preach again. At that point we discovered that he had developed an addiction to certain sexual practices and had, for many years, anonymously visited prostitutes and indulged his addiction.

This may be a rather extreme case of personality inflexibility that often leads to addictions. But let us not delude ourselves. Even the best among us has the potential to turn a compulsive tendency or personality into an addiction. We need all the grace, power, and self-honesty God can give us to keep us from falling. Compulsions and obsessions can mask feelings of anger, hate, loneliness, or rejection. Overcoming our obsessive and compulsive tendencies takes a little effort—but it can be done if we address them honestly and early in our lives.

OVERCOMING OBSESSIONS AND COMPULSIONS

As you will have noticed, obsessions and compulsions, though distinctively different, often go hand in hand. Even in the severest forms of this disturbance, the obsessive-compulsive disorders, they are linked together.

Actual obsessive-compulsive *disorder* requires professional help. Self-help—or treatment by inadequately trained lay counselors or pastors—is likely to reinforce the problem, not cure it.

But what about the "normal" obsessions and compulsions that we all experience? They are amenable to self-help strategies, and the following may be helpful:

1. *Get feelings out in the open.* Since obsessions and compulsions serve either to mask or resolve our deep feelings of anger, rejection, loneliness, or hurt, it is essential to get such feelings out in the open where they can be discussed, felt, and changed if necessary. It is *imperative* that you be able to talk about your feelings. Ask a close friend to help if you don't have a pastor or counselor to talk to. Talk to God about your feelings, too; he will listen.

2. *Work at accepting your negative and painful feelings.* Don't bury your hurts, and don't try to avoid them. Burying pain because you don't like the feeling or denying your anger because you don't believe you should get angry will only give you more reason to continue your obsessive or

compulsive tendencies or perhaps to develop an addiction. Accepting your negative feelings as a fact of existence opens the door to healing.

3. *Allow yourself to feel your pain or hurt.* Cry if you must cry. Be sad if you feel sad. This is a step beyond just accepting your feelings. If you feel depressed, allow yourself to be depressed. In this way you cooperate with God's purposes in these feelings. God created our emotions so that our hurting can bring healing.

4. *However, don't wallow in self-pity.* Self-pity is a form of self-punishment, and wanting to punish ourselves is characteristic of most neurotic tendencies. Give it up. You can be sad without being self-pitying. Just accept and feel your feelings; don't use them to punish yourself.

5. *Change your irrational thinking.* Work at developing healthy forms of thinking. Most people with obsessive and compulsive tendencies have created, over the years, an impaired way of thinking. Their faulty beliefs feed their obsessions, and this impaired thinking in turn creates their compulsions.

The best way I know to straighten out your thinking is to have a close, healthy friend to share your thinking with. Sometimes a spouse can be this friend, but not always. The closeness of the marriage relationship does not always allow for patience, and shared intimacies are sometimes used as weapons between spouses. Make sure, therefore, that you have good communication in your marriage before you share very intimate thoughts.

6. *Finally, don't be afraid to share your intimate problems with God.* Most of us have too narrow a view of prayer. Too often we see it only as "asking" or occasionally "thanking," not as a "sharing" of deep intimacies with God. I am convinced that he is the best listener of all. If you really open up and begin to share, he will show you things about yourself you would never have discovered any other way.

When you pray in a way that is deeply transparent, keep a

journal of your thoughts. (Make sure this journal is kept private; you may want to keep it in a locked drawer.) As you write down your thoughts and review your notes later, you may well be surprised at what God reveals to you. After all, he is the one who knows us better than anyone else. Do you remember the words of King David?

> O LORD, thou has searched me, and known me.
> Thou knowest my downsitting and mine uprising,
> thou understandest my thought afar off.
> Thou compassest my path and my lying down,
> and art acquainted with all my ways.
> For there is not a word in my tongue, but, lo,
> O LORD, thou knowest it altogether. Ps 139:1-4

PART II

Varieties of
Hidden Addictions

SIX

Lifestyle Addictions

C AN AN ENTIRE CULTURE BE ADDICTED?
It's an intriguing question. And in some ways, of course, the answer has to be no. But in the sense that an addiction is an out-of-control, illogical search for pleasure or relaxation at all costs—even to the extent that we risk destroying ourselves and those around us—I believe it is fair to say we're all junkies, every last one of us!

Never before in our culture has there been more affluence, materialism, and waste than in the past ten or twenty years. Our greedy consumption of everything from aluminum to oil and our contamination of the environment from the sea to the outermost layers of ozone are literally destroying the world God created for us. We eat so much that we have to spend $32.6 billion on dieting and diet-related products— fifty-four percent more than the United States government spent on food assistance programs for the poor in 1987. And to a great extent our affluent lifestyle, with its emphasis on buying and possessing as much as we can, lies behind this impoverishment of our world.

"Who, me—affluent?" you may say. "I'm not rich." But affluence is relative, of course. When you compare yourself with your neighbor you may very well feel impoverished. When you look down at smart houses and sleek cars from the window of the bus, you may feel deprived. But try comparing yourself with the rest of the world. To someone whose home is a cardboard box or a tin shanty in some squatters' camp, an apartment, no matter how tiny, looks like a palace. By world standards our society, even with its problems of poverty, is rich.

Tony Campolo, professor of sociology at Eastern College, challenges us to think about our relative affluence and the greed that flows from it in his book *Seven Deadly Sins*. He cites some startling statistics.[1] Eighty percent of the dogs in the United States kept as pets are overweight, while one billion people in the rest of the world go to sleep hungry each night. Forty thousand people die of starvation *each day*, and more than one hundred thousand children go blind every year due to a lack of vitamin A in their diets.

The extent of our more, more, more lifestyle is graphically illustrated by the size of our garbage problem. We junk seven million cars each year—seventy thousand of them are abandoned on the streets of New York City. We throw fifty-two billion aluminum cans and twenty-four billion bottles away each year. By any standard this is disgraceful!

Now, it's one thing for secular society to behave this way, but Christians ought to know better! We have the responsibility of bringing a kingdom perspective to a society of greed and consumerism. And we ought to develop a lifestyle that is Christian in all its choices—from the way we love other people to the way we handle our trash to the way we respond to TV ads. Christians ought to know, better than others, that happiness is not found in possessing more, more, more, but in appreciating what you already have— that contentment, not desire, is the road to happiness.

Unfortunately, all too often, we're part of the problem rather than part of the solution. Christian believers are often as guilty of this greed and waste as anyone. We need God's healing for our addictive lifestyles just as much as the secular culture around us does.

AFFLUENT AND OVERSTIMULATED

Now, the real problem is not the affluence, of course, but what we do with it—and what it does to us. Addiction lurks in our excesses, and until we address and make changes in our lifestyle and abuse of the excess, we will never be free of risk for hidden addictions.

Our relatively high standard of living has a profound effect on the development of *tolerance* for stimulation. The term *tolerance* refers to the way the mind and body gradually become accustomed to a substance or behavior. They "get used to it"; it loses its ability to create a certain mood or take pain away. Another term for this effect is *habituation*; a given stimulus becomes a "habit" that we no longer notice.

Now, our relatively affluent lifestyle, with its movies, TV, restaurants, cars, and other symbols of our high standard of living, violently stimulates our senses. We are bombarded almost continuously with exciting activities, tasty food, and demanding challenges. Just driving five miles on a modern freeway provides as much stimulation as our ancient ancestors got in a whole year. Imagine what a lifetime of stimulation does to us in comparison with earlier times!

This overstimulation of our senses, from noisy music in our cars to rich food in our stomachs, makes us gradually *less* sensitive to stimulation. Our *tolerance* for this bombardment increases; we *habituate* to it, so that gradually we lose our "feel" for it. We become less aware of the stimulation, so we need *more* stimulation just to give us contrast.

Over the years, therefore, our culture has picked up its pace. Music has gotten louder, for instance. High powered radios displaying a bass-frequency responsiveness that shakes the marrow in your bones and costing more than the trucks or vans in which they are installed ply the streets of every city. But it's not just the music, of course. TV commercials have become more dramatic, entertainment more bizarre. With every election, political campaigns seem to sink to a new low of mud slinging and sensationalism. It's the only way they can get the attention of a satiated culture.

This development of *tolerance* to the stimulation of our modern lifestyle is a major contributing factor in the development of hidden addictions. The more we have, the more we must get to keep the stimulation novel. At the same time, even as we become habituated to the overstimulation of our senses, our bodies are reacting to the stress of too much. Thus our drives for pleasure seeking (both stimulation and tension reduction) remain in high gear, making us especially prone to addiction.

A tongue in cheek report in a recent *Newsweek* illustrates this.[2] Gwinn Owens, a retired editor and columnist for the *Baltimore Sun*, dramatically illustrates the kind of ridiculous obsessions and compulsions (and hence addictions) our high-octane lifestyle can lead to. He writes about a friend who, on the way home from work, swings into a shopping mall. In the vast, herringboned parking area of the mall, there are hundreds of empty parking spaces, but the nearest available one is at least a forty-second walk from the door of the store he wants to patronize. So this typical American shopper begins a quest to find the closest possible space.

He first observes the rows of spaces close to the store, probably not more than twenty-five steps away. He stops to wait for a departing Mercedes, hoping that he can slip quickly into the vacated spot. He revs his engine to tell the driver he's waiting—but she doesn't move. The reluctant departer rummages through her packages, brushes her hair, and puts on lipstick. He gets impatient. Traffic is piling up behind him in the lane. Another driver hits the horn and the first driver turns and glares at him. Finally his impatience gets the better of him; he speeds forward into a space reserved for the handicapped. "Just for a moment," he says to his conscience.

Gwinn Owens calls this familiar quest for the nearest possible spot "parking addiction," and he believes it afflicts more Americans than the common cold. Now, I would hesitate to actually call it an addiction, but it comes close. Americans seem obsessed with the idea that parking within ten steps of their destination is their constitutional right. Defying all logic and common sense (the search for the perfect parking spot could easily take much longer than walking from the available space) motorists pursue the "close-in" parking space as a matter of life and death. And this daily obsession may well shorten lives; the anger, acrimonious jockeying, backing, sneaking in ahead of others, honking, shouting, and silent name calling are the basic tools of that silent killer I call stress disease (see chapter 10).

PROBLEM LIFESTYLES

As I have shown, lifestyle and addiction go together. This means we need to challenge our lifestyles—today, more than at any time in our past. And this applies not only to our culture in general, but also to individuals. What specific individual lifestyles are particularly conducive to addictions? There are probably as many "problem lifestyles" as there are types of addictive behaviors. I will focus on the four I consider to be the most common. They all have links to our overarching affluent lifestyle.

Shopping for Stimulation. Peter is a loving and gentle husband. He is generous to a fault, and will do anyone a favor. He has a serious hidden addiction, however. He is a shopping addict. He loves to buy things—it doesn't really matter what. His buying sprees come in cycles. Usually they start when he is depressed or needing some stimulation, because his buying serves as a stimulant.

Peter's compulsive buying began when he earned his first paycheck. He had grown up in a family that was fairly poor and he had become envious of the possessions of others. So when he began earning money as a teenager he started to acquire possessions of his own. At first he frequented garage sales, looking for "bargains." He quickly moved up to discount stores and then department stores, spending every spare cent on advertised bargains.

In the process Peter became a masterful rationalizer. All old-fashioned toys became "collectors' items." Complete sets of tools became "investments." After he married, he began to buy stereo equipment, records, tapes, and videos. Every room in his house became a storeroom.

Compulsive buying gradually became part of Peter's personality. He just had to have everything his eyes saw. And it didn't matter whether he needed the merchandise or not; "owning" was more important to him than "using."

I can understand how Peter's problem developed; at times in my life, I have been something of a compulsive shopper myself. My fascination with certain hobbies began very early in my life, and my cycles of craving have usually followed my shifting hobby interests. Cameras, electronic gadgets, tools, computers, hobby tools for jewelry making (to name but a few)—I doubt if I can ever own enough of these. I am also very aware that tension or depression can stimulate my need for a "fix," and that it would be very easy to get into the habit of buying something to lift my spirits or calm me down through some distraction.

Now using shopping this way is not only expensive; it's clearly unhealthy—and it can lead to addiction. Purchasing sprees only provide temporary stimulation or tranquillity. Like all addictions, you can never get enough of it since it quickly habituates.

Preventing a compulsive shopping tendency from becoming an addiction takes some courage and much self-understanding and self-talk. To know your feelings and recognize when your tension is building is essential. Once you know what is happening you can take steps to intervene. Sometimes I talk myself out of buying something by reminding myself that twenty minutes after I've bought the object of my desire, I will be wanting something else. As a compromise, sometimes I buy something very inexpensive—just as a "token." I might, for example, treat myself to a good book when I've been eyeing a new video player or a new tie when I've been craving a new camera. True, I now have a good library and a substantial collection of ties, but I reckon that's better than spending more than I can really afford! Of course, you can't do this always and in the long run you should bring your compulsive tendency under control.

The bottom line is this: Find the source of your tension and deal with it directly, not by developing a shopping addiction.

Thriving on Chaos. Some people have a lifestyle that can only be described as chaotic. They are disorganized. They experience conflict with family, friends, neighbors, and fellow workers on an almost daily basis. Their life is full of hassles because they don't plan ahead. Their car is always breaking down at the most inconvenient times because they never do preventive maintenance. Murphy's law seems to haunt them; the day after they forget that their householder's insurance is due to be paid, they get robbed.

People like this thrive on chaos (or at least that's how it seems on the outside). Sometimes they are actually addicted to it. The disorder in their lives and its unpredictable results provides a level of excitement that somehow protects them from the serious side of life—the side of responsibility and accountability. They actually find that being disorganized and "harum-scarum" helps them avoid anxiety. Planning and preparation induce too much worry, so they catch-as-they-can.

Parents of teenagers may think this description sounds familiar. Teenagers are notoriously chaotic, partly for the reasons given above. Many teenagers fear responsibility; it causes too many worries. So they prefer to let things slide, and the pay-off is in fact a greater—if temporary—tranquillity. If everything is chaotic, then one more problem isn't even noticed.

Fortunately, for most people, the chaos of the teenage years eventually passes away. If it doesn't, however, the soil for an addiction is fertile indeed.

What can you do to reduce chaos in your life? There are no easy solutions. Since the chaos may be a way of avoiding the anxiety of responsibility and accountability, you may need to seek professional counseling to uncover and confront this anxiety. Lesser chaotic tendencies can be overcome by learning to be more assertive, to organize your time, and to focus your life.

Procrastination. Procrastination can become a lifestyle. It is a habit that is counterproductive to a fulfilling life—and it can easily become addictive.

Most of us are *situational* procrastinators. By this I mean that we don't procrastinate on everything—only on some things. We put off balancing the checkbook but have no problem finding time for a movie. We delay unpleasant tasks like confronting someone we supervise but quickly deal with debts not paid to us. We each have a unique set of situations in which we are most likely to procrastinate. It may be human to err, but it is definitely human to delay!

What are some of the reasons for delaying?

- *Old-fashioned laziness.* This may account for some procrastination, but in my experience it is not the major one.
- *Indecisiveness.* This is getting closer to the bone. We are fearful or uncertain about the outcome of our action, or we fear making a mistake.
- *Ignorance or confusion about how to set about doing what needs*

to be done. If we are unsure about how to balance a checkbook, for example, we are likely to put off doing it.

- *Complexity or unpleasantness of the task.* It may be awkward or associated with some unpleasantness. Conflict with people will often cause us to put off doing something.
- *Personal reasons.* You may feel that life is a long series of obligations that cannot be met, or you generally feel unfulfilled, frustrated,or depressed—not up to tackling a problem.

Now, I am certainly not advocating a "get it all done *now*" kind of compulsiveness. Some things *can* be put off until tomorrow. Repainting the guest bedroom or sorting through some overcrowded drawers may well be able to wait until next year (or not be done at all); matters of life and death don't hang on these actions.

Sometimes it's even prudent to delay rather than act too quickly. You may be too angry to see things clearly, for instance, or you may not have all the facts you need to make a decision. "Sitting" on an issue for a few days often helps clarify thinking and buys time to explore alternatives.

But when you fear that you are unable to do the job, or when your dislike of a job or the order of your priorities puts other lesser demands ahead of what really needs to be done, you rob yourself of real fulfillment. You also set yourself up for serious consequences. A will not completed, for example, could cause much hardship for family and friends. An unreconciled tiff could destroy a friendship.

Some procrastination is necessary for a balanced life. But procrastination becomes a serious problem when it becomes an all-encompassing way of life. When you become a habitual procrastinator, you till the soil of your life for an addiction. Not only do issues pile up when you put them on the back burner, your priorities start to change as well.

When you consistently avoid life and refuse to engage reality, you gradually turn your priorities upside down. When you defer some action, you go into denial; you deceive your mind into thinking it's not important. And this causes problems and pain for you, and for those who love you—as well as for those who wait for your response.

How should you deal with your tendencies to delay?

1. *Try to understand why you procrastinate and what situations trigger it.* Explore the fears, dislikes, hostility, or feelings of inadequacy that cause you to delay. Talking your problem over with a trusted friend can help you pinpoint what causes you to delay. Label it honestly for what it is.

2. *Realize that not all decisions are equally important.* Many issues in life do not have a "right" and a "wrong." You could probably flip a coin and abide by that decision because the outcome is a matter of opinion, not of fact. "Should I buy the green dress or the blue dress?" Neither is absolutely the *right* color. Learn to take risks and be willing to live with your decision. Whether you choose the blue dress (or shirt, or car) or the green one, make your decision right and stop doubting yourself.

I remember seeing a cartoon some years ago in a leadership training manual. It showed a slightly balding executive sitting on a stool with a box on either side of him. The one box was labeled "large" and the other box "small." In front of him was a huge pile of potatoes, and he was holding one of them. His face had a baffled look on it because *all the potatoes were the same size.* Poor fellow; I know how he felt! But life is like that. Many problems are only problems of perception—not of fact. Often, when you have to make a decision, all the potatoes are the same size! Choose one and be done with it.

3. *Never force yourself to make a decision until you feel you have all the facts.* It is usually more dangerous to act without sufficient knowledge than to slow down the process while information is being obtained. But once you have all the information, *decide* and don't procrastinate. Try keeping a list

of decisions that need to be made. As you make them, cross them off the list. If you find that some of them remain too long on the list, then give attention to getting the information you need.

Workaholism. I've already mentioned workaholism several times in this book, and I'll mention it in some more depth in the pages to come, because it is one of the most pervasive of all the hidden addictions. Our Protestant work ethic, despite its many blessings, also has a few curses. When combined with other unhealthy lifestyle practices, it helps to create a deadly addiction.

Workaholism, in fact, probably deserves a chapter to itself. I am discussing it here because it is very much a "lifestyle" problem. Fortunately, much has already been written about this malady, so its nature and symptoms are well-known in our culture.[3, 4]

The term *workaholism* describes an addiction that goes far beyond hard work and long hours on the job. A conscientious and hardworking employee or entrepreneur is a great prize to any community. We often call such people workaholics when, in fact, they are only hard workers. The *true workaholic* has the following characteristics:

- *The workaholic is not free.* Workaholics are unable to play; goofing off creates intolerable guilt feelings. Workaholics also adjust poorly to forced idleness. They are continually compelled by inner forces to work excessively, and often they do not understand these forces.
- *The workaholic depends entirely on his or her work as a source of self-esteem.* Without working, these people consider themselves worthless. They have little social life.
- *The workaholic is totally immersed in work.* People with this addiction have a one-track mind. There is no room in their lives for recreation, hobbies, or community interests. Frequently they experience a "weekend

depression" or "holiday depression." In other words, when forced to relax, the lowered adrenaline causes depression.

- *The workaholic has a neurotic need to work, as opposed to a genuine desire to be gainfully employed.* The neurotic element has to do with proving something to the self. Nothing done seems good enough. The "drivenness" of the workaholic is invariably tied to meeting some unconscious need—such as a need for personal security or for affirmation.

We can easily overdiagnose workaholism. Unlike many other addictions, both substance and hidden, work is necessary. It is also morally good, while many other addictions are morally suspect, if not downright immoral. Hard work is gratifying, even wholesome. When we are physically and mentally healthy, we enjoy work and thrive on it. It can produce neurotic complications, however, if it becomes all-encompassing. In fact, if it is applied to separate, unconscious needs it can become destructive. Voracious inner cravings, irrational fears of failing, and a compulsive drivenness can all take work beyond the bounds of normality and place it in the realm of the addictions.

Just like alcoholism or any other drug addiction, therefore, workaholism can have *many* motives:

- a search for self-aggrandizement,
- an obsession with money and wealth,
- a way of escape from a nagging spouse,
- a need for self-punishment.

This last motive is relevant to much of what goes on in Christian service. Often, because we often feel hypocritical and guilty for not measuring up to what we believe is God's standard for us, Christians unconsciously engage in self-punishment. One way of doing this is to become excessively devoted to doing one's duty—a phenomenon often seen in pastors and missionaries.

How can workaholism be treated? Here are some suggestions. (This process, with some details changed, can serve as a general model for overcoming all hidden addictions.):

1. *Own up to the fact that the workaholism is a problem.* As in all addictions, there is usually a high degree of denial. The addict will consider himself or herself normal or even justified. If you are a hard worker and have been accused of workaholism, listen. Pray and ask God to help you to be honest with yourself. And ask the opinion of several people who know you well. But be careful about asking your boss; he or she may have a vested interest in your workaholism.

2. *Don't minimize or excuse your workaholism.* Once you move beyond denial, you may want to *rationalize* it. "The reason I work so hard is that my wife and kids spend too much." "I think that idleness is sinful and God expects us to be productive." Workaholics can be very creative in coming up with reasons (or excuses) for their excessive devotion to work. It may help to see this devotion as a form of idolatry. Ask God to free you from it.

3. *Identify the harmful aspects of your work addiction.* Write them down! Discuss them with your spouse or a close friend. The more you understand the harmful consequences (to your health or relationships), the easier it will be to change your lifestyle. Your "cure" depends on your ability to recognize that you are missing out on the best things in life. Your family may be suffering because you are so preoccupied with your work. Consider their feelings in this process. Once again, pray and ask God to give you wisdom here.

4. *Change your habits.* Write a contract with yourself for how you will break up your day, week, month, and year. Plan when you will work and when you will relax or play. You may need to cultivate some healthier activities for your "off"

times—like playing tennis, going to the gym, or taking your family on picnics. (But beware of getting into very competitive games; they could meet the same need for stimulation your work does and therefore perpetuate the addiction.) Ask those who are affected by your addiction what *they* would like you to do—for them and for yourself. Ask God to empower you for these changes.

5. *You may need to get professional help.* The root of your problem may be some deep-seated neurotic need. Excessive compulsiveness, competition, or feelings of inadequacy may need to be addressed and your hidden motives uncovered. Slavery to unconscious needs is the worst form of slavery, but becoming the master of these needs will free you to be a whole person. Pray and ask God to direct you to the right help.

I should add one more thought here: don't become a "therapy junkie." It is easy for workaholics to apply the same obsessional tendencies to their therapy that they do to their work. Therapy is intended to help you break free from a lifestyle of dependency, not to become one itself. While some problems may need long-term help, most of them can be solved simply by making the right choices and sticking with them.

AVOIDANCE OF BOREDOM

On several occasions throughout this book I have referred to our constant need for stimulation and our avoidance of low arousal. In an overstimulated society like ours, the absence of stimulation switches off our flow of adrenaline, with unpleasant consequences: we go into depression and experience the withdrawal symptoms of lowered adrenaline. I will focus on adrenaline addiction itself in a later chapter. My focus here is on the deeper "lifestyle" issue that causes us to avoid periods of lowered arousal at all costs.

Boredom, in essence, is a negative emotional response to the "down times" of life. It is a problem faced more by the affluent than the deprived. It is seen more in adults than children, more in the healthy than the sick. Boredom is also a major cause of marital disruption and underlies many marriage break-ups: "I'm bored with you. I need someone new who can excite me."

Boredom is a state of dissatisfaction, frustration, and restlessness. The victim feels a painful emptiness and often cannot identify the real source of this feeling. The days are long and tedious. Time seems to stand still. Most bored people tend to blame circumstances or other people for the problem. "It's my lousy husband." "It's my stupid friends." "It's my miserable job." Hardly ever does the bored victim say, "You know, the problem really is me. It's my attitude and behavior that create my boredom." Pity! If the bored person would own up to the real cause, the boredom would be well on the way to getting resolved.

Boredom is related to addictions because it creates a desire for escape or for stimulation—and both these needs are precursors to addiction. Bored people are at great risk for trying to escape their emptiness and loneliness by establishing an addiction. Alcoholics and drug addicts often start drinking or taking drugs to escape boredom. Workaholics immerse themselves in work to avoid it. Thrill seekers participate in dangerous activities to combat it. Sexual addicts become promiscuous or have affairs, and gamblers head to the casinos or racetracks—all, at first, to avoid being bored. And these are just the "big bad ones." The rest of us become engrossed in lesser addictions. We eat too much, buy too much, and collect too much—all in an attempt to escape boredom.

Perhaps the most favored pastime of the bored is the pursuit of pleasure—both trivial and major. Bored people become country club addicts, golf addicts, movie addicts, and restaurant addicts. They buy sports cars when a sedan will do, purchase sailboats they can't afford, and collect closets full of clothes and shoes. They go to every social event to which they are invited—and to some to which they are not.

The bored person, at root, is *searching for meaning*. When you have everything (or most things) but you're not satisfied, the problem has to be somewhere near the center of your being. When the most fantastic party or the greatest cruise or the most up-to-date gadget doesn't give pleasure that lasts beyond the next morning, then the problem is in the core of your being.

The *real* cure for boredom, then, is to be found in reestablishing the core of your being in a richer soil. As a Christian, I believe that Christ is that "soil." When you are planted or "rooted" in Christ, times of inactivity take on a new meaning. Rather than being a source of negativity and pain, the times of lowered stimulation bring rest to an overused body and restoration to overused glands. They nurture creativity, allowing time and space for ideas to germinate and sprout. They protect us in times of grieving and help us detach from that which is lost to us.

Most important, times of lowered arousal provide an opportunity to "tune into God." In Scripture, communion with God is always associated with *stillness*. "Be still, and know that I am God," advises the psalmist (Ps 46:10). Paul tells the Thessalonians that they should "study to be quiet" (1 Thes 4:11), and Peter advocates cultivating "a meek and quiet spirit, which is in the sight of God of great price" (1 Pt 3:4). To know God in these moments is to sample heaven. It makes it possible to endure suffering and transcend the temporariness of this life—and to live in peace and fullness in the midst of an overstimulated, addictive culture.

SEVEN

Codependency: Addiction to Helping

MILDRED IS AN ATTRACTIVE, intelligent, and dynamic mother of three daughters. At forty-five years of age she retains a youthful zest for life. For the past ten years she has been extremely successful in the business she started when her husband, a pastor, experienced a major depression.

I have seen Mildred as a patient, on and off, for the past ten years. Despite her great competence in the business world, she struggles at times to understand what is going on in her personal life. Since she serves as a consultant to others in her line of work, she sees it as common sense that she should consult a professional for personal issues. In fact, this openness to confront herself and willingness to be transparent about her struggles have been her great strength, even in her business. People know where they stand with Mildred. She seldom "plays games" in her relationships, and her reputation as a person of integrity has spread throughout her church and the business community.

Mildred has one great weakness; she is a great "rescuer." That's good news for anyone who needs to be rescued, but bad news for Mildred. It all became obvious when her husband went into his depression ten years ago. He had accepted the invitation to be pastor of a large church near Los Angeles, mostly because Mildred had encouraged the move. She had been dreaming about starting her own business, and the church's location was ideal for her purposes. But after just one year of ministry the husband realized that he was "bombing out." Major conflicts had developed between himself and senior church leaders over differences in expectations for the church, and he had begun to realize that his ministry there would always be thwarted. Depression set in—a deep, dark melancholy that kept him in bed most days.

Mildred came to the rescue and took her husband to therapy—which is how I first met them. She also ran interference for him at the church. When he couldn't make a meeting, she'd substitute for him and present some excuse for his absence. When he couldn't complete an assignment (like writing his personal "reflections" for the weekly church bulletin), she completed it for him. She even took responsibility for his depression and began to blame herself for their situation.

For more than a year Mildred rescued her husband at every opportunity, despite my suggestion that by doing so she was not helping her husband get out of his depression. Finally the depression lifted, and they moved to another church.

About a year ago I started to see Mildred more regularly in therapy. She wanted to talk about her father who, in his late sixties, was now divorced and living by himself. For most of his life, Mildred's father has had a drinking problem. Mildred left home at age seventeen because she could not stand the conflicts at home that the drinking caused, and for a long time she was able to remain detached from her parents' problems. Now she was becoming hooked again.

"Suddenly," she told me, "it dawned on me why I am always rescuing people. I think I am codependent. I get hooked by other people's problems, especially if they're close to me; and I become obsessed with controlling their behavior."

Mildred, like so many people today, has gotten caught up in what is now being called the "codependency movement." She's read all the books and believes she now has the final explanation for all her problems. But just having a label for what's wrong with her gives her confidence she can overcome it.

Has she found the answer? I doubt it very much. Mildred is just groping for any explanation she can find to explain her behavior. Yes, she has some tendency to be codependent, but no, this doesn't explain all of her behaviors. Unfortunately, many are looking for answers that are too simple, as we will see as we examine the idea of codependency.

THE CODEPENDENCY MOVEMENT—FAD OR FACT?

The codependency movement is a loose network of self-help groups that apply concepts derived from Alcoholics Anonymous (AA) and family systems theory to explain a wide diversity of problems from bad habits to unhealthy relationships. This movement, which is quick to attach the label of "addiction" to every nuance of human behavior, has been very loose in defining its terms and vague in attributing blame for every human failing on someone else's alcohol or drug addiction.

Let me hasten to add: There is a legitimate phenomenon we can call codependency. I have no doubt that *some* family members of chronic alcoholics develop a syndrome in which they are totally controlled by the alcoholic's addiction and therefore become codependent. But I believe we may be taking the idea too far and blaming too many of our personality foibles on one simple dynamic if we label any relative of an alcoholic or a chronic "people helper" as codependent.

There are *many* reasons why someone like Mildred becomes a rescuer. I see as many people with so-called codependency symptoms who come from nonalcoholic families as I do from alcoholic families. *Caretakers* are everywhere, and this is not necessarily bad. To be overly involved in a needy person's life may at times be unhealthy, other times a legitimate expression of sacrificial love. But most important of all, we cannot see codependency as a form of addiction no matter how closely it is tied to an addiction like alcoholism.

One of the reasons why the label *codependent* sounds so plausible as an explanation for problems family members of alcoholics develop is that the description of symptoms given is so generic and comprehensive that *no one escapes the net.* Almost everyone I know who has read the list of symptoms says, "That's me." If it encompasses so many of us, then the syndrome has nothing to set it apart from other problems.

According to the codependency movement literature, almost any compulsive behavior can count as a symptom of codependency—including the "compulsion to caretake, control, work, or eat pecan pies."[1] One popular book on codependency, for example, presents a checklist of more than two hundred characteristics in fifteen categories[2]—and the author then states that this list is *not* "all-inclusive."

I really think this carries the idea too far. I know of no other syndrome that has two hundred characteristics (with more to come) except the syndrome of "being human." I fear that many advocates of codependency may have just found a new label for modern civilization.

In her latest book, this same author concedes that in spite of the emergence of the word *codependency,* it is still jargon.[3] No standard definition exists, nor has anyone agreed on whether it is a sickness, a condition, or a normal response to abnormal people.

As a report in a recent *Christianity Today* article points out, one of the most disconcerting aspects of the codependency movement is the freedom with which the label "disease" is bandied about.[4] Building on the concept that alcoholism is a disease, the concept is also being applied to a host of other behaviors. Eating disorders, obsessions, overworking, and every imaginable compulsion is being called a "disease," and everyone who is or has been around an alcoholic is "codependent." This includes therapists, counselors, ministers, colleagues, and the family.

My word! Just at a time when psychologists are seriously considering reexamining the appropriateness of the "disease" concept of alcoholism, it has jumped the firebreak and is off and burning everything in its path. Clearly we need to pause and reconsider what it is we are talking about when we use the label *codependent*. We need to set some limits and define it more clearly so that those who really have a problem with it can get help, while those whose problems have other causes will not be misdirected.

THE ESSENCE OF CODEPENDENCY

Codependency originally meant "a need to be needed by an addict"—to be a "dependent person's rescuer." Codependents, for various reasons, tend to attach themselves to problems and problem people. The phenomenon was first observed among the families of alcoholics, and the first codependency groups were formed to help the adult children of alcoholics (ACOA) cope with their problems. These groups have been tremendously helpful in freeing those who have been emotionally damaged by the chaos of an alcohol-dominated home. Unfortunately, however, I believe this early connection with alcoholism has served to obscure the real basis of the phenomenon called codependency.

It is widely recognized that the families of alcoholics in particular, but also of addicts in general, often develop a "system" that revolves around the alcoholic. Many family members unwittingly protect or even "enable" the alcohol abuse, thus becoming codependent. But even if some family members unwittingly "collude" with the addict, others don't. Somehow they manage to remain sufficiently detached to be nonanxious and do not get caught up in the crazy world and manipulations of the alcoholic. They don't become codependent and never surrender their control of themselves.

This, I believe, is a major point the codependency movement often overlooks: 1. *Exposure to an addict does not necessarily cause codependency.* A lot depends on how long you've been exposed to the alcoholic influence, how dysfunctionally the family responded to the drinking, your own coping resources, and the amount of support you received from others at the time. I know many people who have grown up in alcoholic homes who are no more codependent than the cat who sat and watched the crazy chaos for years. They are healthy and able to achieve their own happiness without any difficulty. And I know others that were not exposed to the drinking problem long enough for it to make any permanent dent in their psyches.

The story of Mildred I described earlier is a case in point. She is definitely a "rescuer." But her father's drinking problem only began when she was sixteen. She tolerated the short exposure to her father's drinking by distancing herself from the family, so that she never really developed any collusion or need to rescue him—or her mother. She differentiated and pulled away, then at seventeen she left home for college, never to live at home again.

If Mildred's problems were not caused by her father's addiction, where did they come from? Although her father didn't start drinking until she was sixteen, the conflict between her parents had started at least ten years earlier. Many times, as a child, Mildred had felt she had to intervene on her mother's behalf. Her neurotic need to rescue her husband (and anyone else who was in trouble) had its origins in this earlier dysfunction of the home—this ongoing conflict within her family.

And this raises a second point often overlooked by the codependency movement: 2. *Other factors besides addiction can set up codependency problems.* In other words, the same crazy dynamics set up by an alcoholic can *also* be set up by a parent's infidelity, workaholism, or chronic depression.

Actually, since these other problems may or may not have an addiction connection, the term *codependent* is really not an accurate description of the problem. We need a better label to describe the problems created by severe conflict, whether addiction-related or not. However, since that term is commonly used and recognized, I will continue to use it to describe the group of behaviors—especially chronic rescuing of needy people—commonly described as codependency.

If addiction in itself doesn't set up codependency, what does? Mildred's story points to what I consider the essence of the problem usually labeled codependency: 3. *Problems of so-called codependency are problems of conflict more than they are problems of addiction.* It just so happens that the families of addicts are often very conflicted. It may or may not surround an addiction. A mother who is obese and a chronic abuser of food may cause as much conflict in a child as a father who is an alcoholic. A father who is unloving and supercritical can easily set up all the destructive conditions that create the so-called codependency phenomenon. In fact, I would go so far as to say that the consequences of the conflicts this father sets up are even *more serious* than if he were a drunkard.

I recall quite vividly one patient (let's call her Cindy) who came to me in a deep depression when she was about thirty-seven years of age. Cindy's husband, a very successful businessman, was also devoted to his wife; he was running around in circles trying to make her happy. But Cindy kept engaging in a variety of self-defeating behavior—compulsive overeating, excessive rumination, and "people rescuing." She came as close as anyone I have seen to the description usually given of a full-blown codependent. And most of her problems were rooted in her relationship with her father.

The difference, of course, is that Cindy's father had never taken a drink in his life. But he was *uncaring, critical,* even *hateful* at times. Despite his position as a church leader, he had very little love in him, and he made life hell for his daughter. The conflicts were horrendous—fights, shouting, name-calling. Cindy never felt loved, never felt valuable— her father's constant criticism severely damaged her self-esteem and left her constantly fearing she would do something wrong. The legacy of pain in Cindy's life was as dramatic as any I have seen in alcoholic homes.

Codependency, or whatever else we want to call this syndrome, is the product of severe conflict. It results when we fail to develop an adequate set of skills for managing conflict. This clarification can help us focus on the real issues of how to cope with it.

All of life is filled with conflict, and all of us have the capacity to develop codependency. As Dr. Edwin Friedman points out, "All human beings are programmed for far more pathology than could possibly become manifest in a lifetime."[5] Our capacity to do things wrong is far greater than our capacity to do things right—humanly speaking. Life is a rough ocean—that is a given. How we sail through the storms it throws at us determines whether we are adaptive or reactive, healthy or neurotic. The modeling of the most important people in our lives, our parents and spouses, can help us choose healthy patterns of behavior, but they are not the sole determiners of how we respond. Conflicts are inevitable, and we must take responsibility for how we handle them.

WHERE DOES LOVE END AND CODEPENDENCY BEGIN?

Much of what is described as codependency is really a "love gone wrong." But I know from my conversation with many who fear that they are codependent that they are confused about when they are being loving and when they are acting out their codependency.

"I don't know what to do anymore," one client told me recently. "My aged mother needs my help. I can't turn my back on her when she asks me to visit her or buy her something, yet because she was an alcoholic for many years I think I've become codependent. Where does love end and codependency begin?"

I can understand this confusion. The codependency movement urges neurotic people-helpers to protect themselves—to stop taking care of others and to start taking care of themselves. Often this is very helpful advice. It exposes many *oppressive* "rules" that codependents tend to internalize—

- Don't think for yourself.
- Don't be aware of your feelings.
- Don't have fun but only do your duty.
- Don't get close to people.
- Don't mature or change.
- Don't trust anyone—not even yourself.

—and urges codependents to "unlearn" them. It encourages greater self-care and a greater awareness of one's own self-worth.

Who can argue with such admirable changes! By every imaginable standard, these qualities of self-care and maturity are healthy. But we must be careful not to throw the baby out with the bath water. If counteracting codependency does not move us to also develop a *healthier way of loving others* (including alcoholic parents), we may find ourselves going from one extreme to the other—from being neurotic caregivers to being uncaring and nonloving. It is a tightrope only God can help us traverse.

Codependency is often described as a problem of relationships—a tendency to get too close to others or become "enmeshed" in the problems of another person. This can cause a lot of confusion. In these troubled times, parents, for example, often need to help their children financially well into their adult years. Is this enmeshment or not? Is there codependency when one person is deeply involved in helping another in time of serious trouble? What must parents do when an adult child turns to them for financial help—turn their backs?

Here again, I think that this confusion can be cleared up if we focus on the conflict theme in true codependency. If *any* relationship creates a problem of conflict, it can set up the conditions for codependency. If getting too close to someone causes you to be manipulated or to act in collusion with some behavior you don't approve of, then the relationship has the potential for codependency. But let us not forget that the love to which God calls us may come awfully close at times to codependency. The line between them is very fine. Love may sometimes command us to become more deeply involved than we feel comfortable with. After all, this is what Christ did for us.

I am convinced that there is a way of preventing codependency from developing in times when one person's need demands sacrificial love from another. That way involves maintaining a close relationship with God and staying sensitive to his promptings and direction. He alone can teach us to love in a healthy way. He can help us maintain healthy relationships with those who are closest to us and to help others without becoming infected with the codependency "bug."

Such a close relationship with God keeps your loving healthy. Like so many good things, love can become sick. Codependency, if nothing else, is a love that has gone wrong. Codependents cannot set boundaries. They cannot be tough when they ought to be tough. They become people pleasers—unable to say "no" to any demand placed upon them. They end up attaching themselves to people and their problems as a way of earning love and respect, not out of true love.

A healthy love, on the other hand, knows where appropriate boundaries are and when to detach itself; it doesn't cling. It can release the object of the love to be itself and doesn't try to solve problems that aren't its to solve.

Healthy love also sees no purpose in trying to prove itself by receiving abuse without complaining. There are many who make this mistake, aren't there? "I had better not tell him that his criticism hurts me because he may think I don't love him," a patient told me recently. Her husband has been cold and indifferent for years. The more he has distanced himself from her, the more she has tried to show her love for him by allowing the various abuses he has meted out. Everything she does only receives his scorn. He compares her with others all the time—criticizing the way she dresses, cooks, and even talks.

I have had to correct this woman's theology. She has always believed it was her Christian duty as a faithful wife to "turn the other cheek." But when I push her to be honest, she admits that deep down she is very angry and resentful. Her dreams are full of hate and revengeful acts toward her husband. Her passive acceptance of abuse, then, cannot be acts of love!

"Turning the other cheek" is an act of profound forgiveness, and we are all called to "forgive our enemies" no matter how much they have harmed us. But love also requires us to be honest. When someone persistently abuses us, it is an act of love to share your feelings with the abuser.

As I began to teach my patient how to be honest in her responses to her husband, a miracle began to happen. He began to change. I taught her to calmly respond to his criticism with "I know I cannot please you in what I do, but your criticism of me hurts very deeply. I would appreciate it if you would stop." When he was verbally abusive, I taught her to say, "I may not be able to defend my actions, but I don't deserve your verbal abuse."

Slowly she became more courageous. Slowly he became more respectful. Together they have begun to build a new relationship. Pretty soon, I suspect, he is going to fall in love with her all over again. This is what a healthy love tends to do in relationships; it clones itself!

CODEPENDENCY VERSUS ADDICTION

Just as there is much confusion about the difference between love and codependency, there is also a lot of confusion about whether codependency is an addiction itself. We know that in classic codependency there is another person who is addicted or dependent on something, usually alcohol or drugs, and the secondary person therefore becomes codependent because of the conflicts generated. The codependent allows the dependent person's behavior to affect him or her and becomes preoccupied with controlling other people's behavior. The alcoholic's destructive behavior is denied or minimized, boundaries are formed to protect the family, and feelings of anger, fear, shame, or depression are suppressed or denied.

But is the codependent also addicted to something? Is it an addiction to helping others or to being needed? Since the need to protect the alcoholic is very strong, roles in the family often reverse: children take on the role of parents, while adults become children. Again and again one hears an adult child of an alcoholic say, "I became his mother. I would tell him when to get up and when to go to bed. I would empty his booze down the drain. I would scold him, love him, hate him, and once I even spanked him. I never had a father—I had a problem child!"

But does this make for an addiction on the part of the child? There is no doubt that one learns certain habits when exposed to a disruptive alcoholic and that certain behaviors become entrenched. When you encounter someone else in need, you are likely to respond in the same way as you did to your dad when he drank. But is a habit necessarily an addiction?

There are those who say yes, who insist that addiction and codependency are practically the same. One writer sums it all up when she states that there exists a basic "generic" disease she calls "the addictive process."[6] This embraces codependency, alcoholism, eating disorders, obsessive-compulsiveness, and even some psychoses. To me, this broad generalization is like saying that all addictions are due to our being human and living in a body full of needs. It's true—but not helpful when it comes to sorting out one need from another.

So, while I reject the idea that all codependency is a form of addiction, I do accept that *some* codependents can be considered to be addicted to their codependency or to some aspect of it. This follows from some of the points I made in the first chapter. Let me review the essential characteristics of an addiction:

- Addictions provide escape from our true feelings.
- Addictions totally control the addict, transcending all logic or reason.
- Addictions always involve pleasure.
- Addictions are destructive and unhealthy.

- Addictive behavior takes priority over all other life issues.
- Addicts deny their addiction.

Clearly, some codependents can meet most of these criteria. To illustrate how difficult it is to call codependency an addiction, I recall working with Anne, a middle-aged, married woman whose elderly mother, a former alcoholic, lived nearby. Anne had become her mother's caretaker long before the mother really needed any caretaking. Being manipulative and controlling, the mother had faked several heart attacks in order to bring Anne scurrying back from a vacation to take care of her. She resented Anne's marriage and at one point actually came out and told Anne that she didn't understand why Anne gave more attention to her husband than to her.

Over many years the mother's persistent nagging had influenced Anne. She came to believe that she was a "wicked daughter." Her self-esteem lay at rock bottom, and her pervasive feelings of guilt were overwhelming. She *had* to do things for her mother like calling her every hour or two, telling her whenever she left the house, doing all her shopping, always admitting she was wrong, never saying no to the mother's demands, and never letting on that she had had fun anywhere else.

Anne's codependency could possibly be called an addiction when she developed a severe ulcer and refused to seek treatment. She feared that her mother would blame herself for the ulcer—and Anne could not tolerate the thought of having her mother in any pain. She was allowing someone else to destroy her and was putting up no resistance—but she denied the problem. The more I tried to reason with Anne, the worse she resisted any change. What is missing to make Anne's codependency unequivocally an addiction is the element of pleasure—unless in some way masochism and self-denial can be interpreted as providing some strange and unexplainable pleasure. Perhaps the word "pleasure" needs to be also understood, in the context of addictions, as a form of self-gratification—whether it is positive or negative.

Finally I got Anne's husband involved and took firm action. Anne was hospitalized. Her mother was initially irritated but soon settled down to accepting the change. She even recovered some self-sufficiency and was able to take a taxi to the hospital to visit her daughter.

A much healthier relationship developed following Anne's release from the hospital. She came to realize what she had been doing and now is able to reason with herself. The addiction is broken, even though some codependency habits still exist. Now that she takes better care of herself and sets limits on what she will do for her mother, everyone is healthier.

CODEPENDENCY AND THE SELF

Problems with the self are very common in codependents. People with this set of problems have low self-esteem. They lose touch with themselves and forfeit any ability to think for, feel for, act for, or take care of themselves. This doesn't necessarily have any connection with addiction, although the codependent could easily develop an addiction or become addicted to his codependency as a way of escaping the pain of his self-problems.

There is also a great deal of "learned helplessness" among codependents. Learned helplessness is the label put on people who come to *believe* they are helpless, even though this may not be true. People with learned helplessness don't believe they can affect the outcome of anything, and therefore they take no action to stop or change an unsatisfactory situation. (This is often the case with victims of abuse and helps explain why they keep "coming back for more.")

Most commonly, codependents come to associate their self-worth with their ability to meet the needs of others. "If I do what my husband wants me to do, I'm a good person. If I don't, I'm no good." In the process three things happen:

- *They abandon all independence.* They become focused not on the other person, but on meeting the *expectations* of the other person.
- *They fail to achieve full autonomy.* They live out their lives as "incomplete" selves. Something is missing. They are only half a self. They never feel complete.
- *They fail to become all that God intends them to be* (see Romans 5:2).

It is almost impossible to live out God's full plan for your life if you are codependent. If you give someone else that much control over you, it is not possible to also give God control over your life.

This is a tension I see in the lives of many pastors and missionaries. There is a sense in which they develop all the characteristics of "codependency" in their relationship with parishioners. Because they lack an adequate sense of self, a clear vision of God's calling, and an adequate understanding of how people, even Christian people, can manipulate others for their own ends, they become neurotic people helpers. And once that has happened, they stop being God's person for that time and place. Do you remember the words of Jesus in Matthew 6:24?

No man can serve two masters: for either he will hate the one, and love the other; or else he will hold to the one, and despise the other. . . .

True, Jesus was talking about serving God while trying to serve "riches," but the same principle applies to surrendering control of our lives to someone else. When we allow someone other than God to determine what we do, where we go, or how we act, we cannot be obedient to God. We are not free to follow his leading.

This has important implications for the problem of codependency. Unless we remain primarily committed to a better understanding of who we are and how God can help us become healthier in the deepest parts of our being, we will tend to have problems with our commitments to people—either fear of commitment or overinvolvement. Unless we keep our dependency entirely Godward, we remain at risk for codependency.

EIGHT

Religious Addictions

A RE CHRISTIANS ESPECIALLY PRONE to hidden addictions? As with so many difficult issues in life, the answer is "yes and no." I wouldn't say that being a Christian in and of itself increases a person's risk of developing a hidden addiction. But those people who become addicted to religious activity might be said to be more prone to hidden addictions because their addictions are so easily hidden! When an activity has a "spiritual" dimension, addiction to that activity easily goes undetected. My purpose here, therefore, is to provide some guidelines for differentiating addictive spiritual activities from healthy ones.

RELIGIOUS FETISHES

It is quite remarkable how a true addiction can masquerade as a legitimate spiritual activity—how the Bible, Christian artifacts such as the cross, and even places of worship can become objects of superstition rather than true expressions of true faith.

When this happens, these objects, places, or activities become *fetishes*. A fetish is an object or practice that is believed to have power in and of itself or that is given irrational devotion. For example, a person who has never personally participated in sports may make a fetish out of a particular team and give it excessive attention and loyalty. A person who has always been poor may make a fetish out of money. In the arena of sexuality, a fetish may be an object such as a shoe or stocking used as an erotic "substitute," the object of sexual devotion.

Almost any aspect of religious life—the Bible, prayer, fellowship, tithing, helping the poor, attending worship services, witnessing to one's faith, and more—has the potential to become a fetish. All these things, while good in themselves and necessary to the ministry of the gospel, can become *substitute* objects of devotion. And because these attachments provide pleasure in the form of stimulation or release from tension, they take on the potential to form an addiction.

I truly believe that this is at the root of modern idolatry. We don't fabricate "graven images" or likenesses of God in our sophisticated society. We don't worship the work of our hands in wood or stone (see Deuteronomy 4:28). But we do worship the work of our hearts—substituting worship of the activities and objects of our faith for worship of God himself (see Romans 1:23). When we do this we turn our "faith" into a "religion" and run the risk of turning our practice of faith into an addiction. Religious addiction is a real phenomenon.

A CASE OF CHRISTIAN ADDICTION

Brought up in a Christian but unhappy and dysfunctional home, Rose was always unsure of herself. When she turned twenty-one, a young man in her church professed deep love to her and proposed marriage. Rose didn't really want to marry the young man, but her parents pressured her into marriage because they believed it was God's will for her life. But five years of marriage and three children later, Rose suddenly came to her senses. Although her husband was a kind and loving man, Rose realized she had never loved him. But she was trapped, because she didn't believe in divorce.

About this time, Rose began to intensify her spiritual activity. At first it seemed that she had experienced a spiritual renewal. She began to carry her Bible everywhere she went—not just to church or prayer meetings, but to the supermarket, PTA meetings, the hairdresser, and the movies.

Eventually Rose's husband noticed that she never *read* her Bible; in fact, she hardly ever opened it. Instead, she treated it like a security blanket. When he tried to take it away from her after she had fallen asleep with it in bed, she would react with fear, grab it back, and put it next to her under the blankets. It was at this point that Rose's husband realized there was more to Rose's attachment to the Bible than a genuine need for its contents. The Bible itself had become a fetish, a substitute object of devotion, and Rose was addicted to the comfort she derived from it. Rose felt trapped in her marriage, and her attachment to her Bible was a way of relieving the discomfort of her feelings, not an expression of genuine religious devotion.

A FAITH TURNED TO ADDICTION

Christians, therefore, are just as capable of turning their faith practices into hidden addictions as non-Christians are in turning work and play into addictions. Why do I say this? Because Christians are human, and this means they:

- need emotional healing,
- are prone to distort their needs,
- may be guilt-ridden,
- don't understand the addictive process.

Calvin Miller, in his book *The Taste of Joy,* warns that many Christians are only "Christaholics" and not disciples at all. He points out that real disciples are cross bearers; they seek to follow the true Christ, not make a fetish of him or any aspect of following him. Christaholics, on the other hand, are escapists who are looking for a shortcut to happiness. They want the joy that comes from knowing Christ but none of the responsibility.

The possibility of religious addiction is something every Christian leader should acknowledge, because in urging others to greater devotion, there is always the danger of encouraging the development of addictions. Given the tremendous emotional needs many in our culture feel, there is always the temptation, in presenting and interpreting the gospel, to overemphasize "what religion can do for you." Our preaching, teaching, and writing, therefore, can lead people down the addiction path rather than the true experience of Christ's path if we unknowingly give too much reverence to the objects of our faith rather than to Christ.

This is not to say, of course, that Christ does not meet needs. But his gospel makes it clear that the way to getting our needs met is to develop a relationship with him, not a dependency on a particular aspect of following him or an attachment to the stimulation of discipleship.

SERIOUS FAITH IS NOT RELIGIOUS ADDICTION

There are those who would be quick to say that *anyone* who is intense about his faith is addicted to that faith. But religious fervor is not the same thing as religious addiction.

Take Sam, for instance. Since he became a Christian six months ago, he has felt a great hunger to "know the Word." He listens to religious tapes while he drives and often falls asleep at home reading the Bible. When he's with friends and family, all he wants to talk about is his faith, Scripture, and how the world needs Christ. He drives his friends up the wall because he doesn't seem interested in anything else.

Now, Sam may possibly be doing a disservice to the gospel by ramming it down people's throats whenever he gets an opportunity, but he is not a "religious addict." Serious religion is not what addiction is about.

At what point does a serious commitment become a religious addiction? To an extent, of course, that is a judgment call. One giveaway is that all the "energy" of the devotion seems focused at one *aspect* of religion rather than at God himself. Another is that the attachment proves destructive to the addict and those around him or her. (Even here, it is necessary to distinguish between what seems destructive and what is truly destructive.) Yet another is the amount of control the person has over his or her activities. Being under the will of Christ never releases us from the obligation of exercising personal responsibility. If a person's religious attachment controls him or her to the degree that control is lost, an addiction may well be suspected.

ADDICTIONS TO RELIGIOUS ECSTASY

If you were to ask me where the greatest risk of addiction masquerading as legitimate spiritual activity lies, I would point to the quest for religious *ecstasy* and *euphoria*. Most Christians avoid addictive substances, but many fall in the trap of searching for relief from the tensions of life through "getting high" on spiritual experiences. The practice of religion can provide an ecstasy that is as potent as any mind-altering drug. Church then becomes not a community for serving God but the source of a weekly or semi-weekly "shot in the arm" or "fix."

The relationship between ecstasy and a true spiritual experience has always intrigued me. Through the years I have encountered many Christians who claim to have had an "ecstatic experience," a trancelike, deeply moving sensory experience. And this may well have been a true spiritual experience. After all, a genuine encounter with God cannot help but have a deep emotional effect on us. But encounters with God are not always—or even usually— "ecstatic." And if we seek him simply to experience a euphoria that overrides our emotionally constricted defenses, we are seeking him for the wrong reason.

My concern, then, is not with emotional feelings about God, but with the *quest* for these ecstatic experiences. For many it becomes an addicting quest. They derive pleasure or release from tension from these ecstatic experiences. For them, religious ecstasy becomes just another "fix." And like so many "fixes," the experience is short-lived and physiologically draining. Our bodies can only take so much of it. The higher the mountain of euphoria, the deeper is the valley of letdown that follows; therefore the process of addiction becomes established very quickly. And because it is associated with a spiritual quest, this kind of hidden addiction is harder to recognize than most.

When my wife and I were dating, we were friends with another couple who had become Christians about the same time as we. We shared many prayer times together and participated in youth rallies and mission activities. But over time, we began to experience friction with them, because their spiritual quest seemed to depend on the search for ecstatic or mystical experiences. Because of their need for spiritual excitement, they could never spend a quiet evening studying Scripture or reading Christian literature; they always had to be "doing" something. They wanted a feeling experience—and there seemed to be no limit to their appetite for religious emotion. The result was that they jumped from church to church and lacked any consistency. After several weeks of worshiping in one place, they quickly became accustomed to it (this is the exact equivalent of how drugs habituate) and needed some new experience to create their next high. So off they went to the next church. Novelty was essential. As soon as a preacher or experience became familiar, it lost its ability to make them euphoric.

After just one year, our friends were burned out. They became disillusioned and went through a period of deep confusion about their faith. At this time my wife and I married and moved away. But reports I have received over the years about our friends' spiritual pilgrimage reveals that they have continued to follow their old patterns of religious addiction.

The quest for religious ecstasy is closely tied with the phenomenon of mysticism. Unfortunately, the word *mysticism* is much abused today and can mean anything from just an unexplained experience to direct communication with God. It is also applied to experiences that are obscure or occult in nature.

Mysticism, in the simplest meaning of the term, is a type of religious emphasis which emphasizes a direct and intimate *awareness* of the divine presence. It is religion at its most intense and emotional form. Many "contemplative" practices, where the focus is on meditation, are designed to create this consciousness.

Many Christians over the ages have reported ecstatic mystical experiences as a part of their spiritual journey. St. Francis of Assisi and St. Teresa of Avila, for instance, spoke of brief times when they were overcome by a burning zeal and total detachment from the self. During such episodes, they experienced a profound sense of God, a deep sense of composure, and a powerful sense of wonder. Certain forms of mystical ecstasy—often called "rapture"—involve a sense of flying or of being borne on eagles' wings or being in flight, followed by an intense consciousness of forgiveness and the revelation of divine secrets. St. Teresa described one such experience as follows:

> All burnt up, the soul is renewed like the Phoenix, and one can devoutly believe that its faults are pardoned. Now that it is so pure, the Lord joins it with himself . . .[1]

It's hard to remain unaffected by the descriptions given by these historical Christians—and by modern ones as well—of mystical and ecstatic religious experiences. Psychologists, especially, have long been interested in these "altered states," Interestingly, most have concluded that such states need not be pathological and may be very positive, producing a unification, not a disintegration, of the personality.

There is no doubt in my own mind that these deep and profound experiences of the presence of God can be both genuine and healthy. When we give ourselves to God in total surrender and provide time for prayer and meditation, we will be deeply moved at times.

But the difference between these mystical experiences which are God-centered and seeking ecstasy is important: the emotional experience was not sought for its own sake, but as a means of coming closer to God. The distinction is one of motive. Addicted Christians want the feelings. Saints want God!

I can see two pitfalls, therefore, in our modern-day preoccupation with ecstasy, and these relate directly to our hidden addictions:

- In many cases the ecstatic experience may simply be a form of *catharsis* for repressed emotions.
- The ecstatic experience is so reinforcing in and of itself that people may seek it for the experience's sake, not

for the communion with God that it is intended to facilitate. To put it simply—our search is for pleasure, not for God.

First then, let me discuss the *catharsis* aspect of ecstasy. One of the dangers of *emotionalism* as we see it evidenced in some Christian circles today is that the heightened emotions that are experienced in worship and prayer may serve merely to purge or release pent-up feelings or tensions. This is not all bad, of course; in these days of high stress and tension, most of us need all the catharsis we can get. But Satan can *also* use emotional catharsis to further his ends and to deceive us into believing we have the genuine article. He does this in New Age religions all the time. There can be *false* charismatic or ecstatic experience that merely relieves tension but doesn't bring us nearer to God. The psychological release may cause us to feel cleaner and more at peace afterwards, but it is a false peace that cannot sustain us. We have to seek it again and again. Eventually, this search can become an addiction.

The word *catharsis* comes from the Greek, meaning "to purge or to clean out." When you take a laxative you "clean out" the digestive system—a physical catharsis. Sigmund Freud, you may recall, developed the technique of psychological *catharsis* in which he used hypnosis to help people reenact emotionally painful situations. The catharsis was supposed to purge the emotional system by allowing the patient to use up all the energy that had been bottled up inside. To some extent it does work!

In every life there are many cathartic opportunities. We go to football games and the theater and even listen to music in order to release emotional tension. Unfortunately, we may also unwittingly turn our religious experiences into nothing more than cathartic experiences. The likelihood of this happening is greater when the mechanism is not understood.

This then leads to the second pitfall: The ecstatic experience—not God himself—can become the focus of our quest.

We all desire to reach the highest level we can on our climb up the spiritual mountain. We want to be the best of all climbers and are open to guidance from those ahead of us on the best route to take. We desire to bring our wills into conformity with God's will and to divest ourselves of every unnecessary burden that will hamper our upward journey. But we are in trouble if we get caught up in the climb itself to the point that we forget where we are climbing! Like a mountaineer who becomes distracted from the climb by the gorgeous scenery or the exhilaration of climbing, we can get sidetracked into thinking that ecstatic religious *experiences* are an end in themselves.

Now, only God knows whether these moments of "high" are truly spiritual experiences or merely psychological mechanisms of catharsis. If God is in the experience, the outcome will always be wholesome and bring healing. My only concern is to remind us that such experiences have the potential to become addicting when we seek them for their own sake rather than as means to the end of encountering God.

ADDICTIONS TO BELIEF

At the beginning of this chapter I pointed out that a true addiction can easily masquerade as a legitimate spiritual activity. This is especially true in the area of beliefs. There is a variation of obsessional thinking in which we use certain religious beliefs as a way of hiding from our true feelings and escaping the anxiety of our existence. We focus on and become obsessed by certain *secondary* and unimportant spiritual ideas in order to avoid facing the real ones.

"The primary theme in the history of the world," the

German poet Goethe once wrote, "is the conflict between belief and unbelief."[2] This is especially true in the Christian life. We believe, and yet we don't believe. We want to believe but can't always maintain our beliefs. Most of us can identify intensely with the prayer of the father whose demoniac son who was brought to Jesus for healing: "Lord, I believe; help thou mine unbelief" (Mk 9:24).

One of the unhealthy ways we can deal with our natural tendency to unbelief on certain issues is to take a very *opposite* position on an issue or point of doctrine and become obsessionally preoccupied with it. We literally become addicted to the belief as a way of shutting out our unbelief.

Every church I have ever known has its "heresy hunters"—those members who feel a self-imposed responsibility to keep the faith "pure." They are on guard for any hint of heresy (as defined by them) and will jump down others' throats or go for the jugular at the slightest provocation. Pastors all over the world confirm my observation that there's at least one in every church. I suspect I may even have played this role myself at times.

In one church I attended years ago, the "heresy hunter" was an early retiree who had worked as a telephone technician. Cedric (not his real name) had no theological training (not always the case with heresy hunters), but he didn't let that stop him from throwing his weight around on matters of belief.

Cedric always sat in the back of the church, in the pew nearest the door. To guarantee getting this seat, he would be at the church long before anyone else. He was even known to have rudely chased out strangers who had unwittingly sat in "his seat." I am convinced that Cedric sat in this position so that he could keep an eye on how others were reacting to the sermon and thus gain ammunition for attacking the pastor later. He would take a count of heads nodded in agreement or shaken in disagreement over statements from the pulpit. The disagreements he would report to the pastor; he seldom reported the affirmations.

He personally caused more headaches, stomach upsets, and ultimately even ulcers or heart attacks for pastors of that church than almost any aspect of congregational life. And all the time he sincerely believed he was the agent of God, keeping apostasy at bay. He carefully scrutinized every sermon for hints of heresy. If the pastor strayed from Cedric's particular view of orthodoxy, Cedric would write a letter of complaint or raise the issue as loudly as possible in front of the church as the pastor was greeting people. He never let an opportunity go by without raising hell.

Most of Cedric's pet "beliefs" were both paranoid and ignorant. In his view, for example, only the King James Version of the Bible was God's inspired Word; he knew nothing about the canon of Scripture or the need to translate the Scriptures from original languages. He also believed that all forms of entertainment were satanic and that God meted out punishment at every opportunity. When someone had a flat tire he would say, "God is punishing you for some sin in your life." When someone else was emotionally down he would say, "God is withdrawing from you to force you into greater obedience." He had a spiritual explanation for all misfortune—and he never hesitated to use those explanations as a club.

All the time I knew Cedric I strongly suspected that he was a man full of unbelief and that his heresy hunting was an unconscious way of keeping his unbelief out of his awareness. And some years later, after we had moved on, I heard that he had given up the faith, divorced his wife of thirty-five years, and run off with a younger woman. My suspicion was confirmed; Cedric's addiction to heresy hunting was his way of relieving the tension of his own doubts.

A mechanism called "reaction formation" is often at work behind addiction to dogmatic and inflexible beliefs or behaviors. Reaction formation is a step beyond denial.

Instead of simply shutting ourselves off from reality, we try to *change* reality, adopting false feelings that are the opposite of our true feelings. If a daughter hates her aged mother, for example, yet cannot face the "unacceptable" feeling, she may practically smother her mother with love. This was what happened in Cedric's case. His doubts were so unacceptable that he reacted by becoming rigidly "believing," not allowing any doubts to enter his consciousness. This then made him the guardian of truth—except that he was not really concerned about truth for truth's sake; he merely wanted to remove anything that would feed his doubts.

Reaction formation has high potential for forming an addiction to certain behaviors because it both keeps us from our real feelings and provides a degree of stimulation. If we are unable to accept our feelings for what they are, we set about obsessionally or compulsively safeguarding our defenses against them. If we cannot face our doubts honestly, as the father of the demoniac boy was able to, then we are likely to engage in beliefs or behaviors that keep us away from these doubts. The need to maintain this avoidance then becomes addicting.

I believe that God wants us to be truthful in our living—to own up to our doubts; our feelings of anger, depression, or hate; and our desires for resentment and revenge. If we don't own up to these feelings before him, we can never come to know the full depth and completeness of his healing. When Jesus said, "Ye shall know the truth, and the truth shall make you free" (Jn 8:32), he was referring primarily to himself as Messiah. I can't help believing, however, that he also meant that the truth about ourselves can liberate us to a fuller and more meaningful spiritual life—thus keeping us from becoming belief addicts.

Hidden addictions are just as capable of distorting the truth about our innermost workings and feelings as any drug or alcohol addiction. Healing from *all* addiction can only come via truth—truth about God, yes, but also truth about ourselves.

THE DYNAMIC CHRISTIAN SPIRITUAL LIFE

The Christian who seeks to grow in an authentic spiritual experience will have to avoid many pitfalls. One of the most vivid and accurate descriptions of these hazards was given in John Bunyan's seventeenth-century classic, *Pilgrim's Progress*, which describes the journey of a character named Christian from the City of Destruction to the Celestial City. On the way, Christian encounters many people and places that would stop his progress. His neighbors mock and threaten and a couple, named Obstinate and Pliable, even try to fetch him back by force. In the Slough of Despond, the burden on his back almost causes him to sink in the mire of depression. And he encounters many other dangers and hindrances before he finally reaches his destination.

But Christian has an experience early in his journey that helps prepare him for the road ahead. At the house of Interpreter, he is taken into a room where two children sit, each in a chair. The eldest is called Passion and the younger one is Patience. Passion is very discontented. Patience is very quiet. Christian asks Interpreter, "What is the reason for the discontent of Passion?" Interpreter tells him that both children have been told to wait until next year before receiving "the best things." Passion is impatient and wants them now. Patience, on the other hand, is content to wait.

Then Christian sees a man come in with a bag of treasure that he pours at the feet of Passion, who jumps for joy and laughs scornfully at Patience for being willing to wait. But after a little while Passion is discontented again. He has squandered his treasure and is left only with rags. Patience is still content to wait.

Christian learns a profound lesson in this encounter—one

that can help us in understanding and overcoming religious addictions. Passion is what this world is all about. It is the "now" generation attitude: I want it *now* and I want it *my way.* People in our culture are always on the search for immediate gratification. But in the end, all they receive are rags.

Patience has the best wisdom. Although he is the younger, he knows that the best is not in this world, but in eternity, and that it is better not to covet things that are "now" but to wait for that which is to come. ". . . For the things which are seen are temporal; but the things which are not seen are eternal" (2 Cor 4:18).

Christian was to discover that the lesson of Passion versus Patience would be a difficult one to remember, but it is one that must be learned well if one is to achieve a dynamic spiritual life. The relationship between *our* passion for pleasure and privilege in this life and the patience needed to keep our final destination in view is an uneasy one. Christians must live in a constant state of tension between the "now" and the "not yet"; we are pulled between relating to this world and keeping our "treasures" in heaven, between meeting the demands for a meaningful and secure existence and realizing that "this too will pass."

My experience as a therapist leads me to believe that too large an investment in the "now" almost invariably leads to some addiction. Practically every hidden addiction you can think of—workaholism, gambling, shopaholism, or over-eating—has its roots in too much preoccupation with "this present world." Such a preoccupation is evidence of un-balanced, unhealthy spirituality and needs to be corrected by the grace of God.

But being preoccupied with eternity to the neglect of this life is unbalanced spirituality, too. It is possible to become so engrossed in your heaven-boundedness that you are of no earthly value! God has created this world and placed us in it for his purposes. For us to tell God we're tired of this life and order him to move us on to eternity would be silly and presumptuous. His response would simply be to point us to the parable of the talents and remind us that he expects us to be faithful stewards of this life (Mt 25:14-30).

Several weeks ago I counseled with a young man who was struggling to live a consistent Christian life and be true to what he believed was God's plan for him. He was also struggling with intense depression over his failures and the overwhelming desire to end his life.

In the middle of our discussion he interrupted me and asked, "Why doesn't God just take us home to be with him? Why do we have to struggle with the failures of this life when he promises something better?"

"I don't know why God expects us to live a life on this earth with its pain and suffering," I replied, "but I do know that in his eternal plan human existence is important. He wants me to live out my life the best I can. You have to take that by faith."

The pain seemed to leave his face. Slowly he smiled back at me.

"You really believe that, don't you?" he said.

I nodded. He nodded back. It was the turning point in his therapy.

What is the hallmark of a dynamic and healthy spiritual life? It is *balance*—and this includes the balance between living now and living in the expectation of eternity. We are to be *in* the world, but not *of* it. We are to enjoy the fruits of this world, but not to let the search for them control us. When we achieve this kind of balance, our likelihood of developing a religious addiction—or any kind of addiction— is very small indeed.

NINE

Addictions
to Sex and Love

T HE MOST POWERFUL FORCE in the physical world is not the
nuclear bomb—but sex! Addictions to alcohol and
cocaine may be major problems for our age, but they pale
into insignificance when compared with the ravages of sex
gone wrong.

This powerful force derives part of its might from the
complex system of hormones that program us to seek
procreation. The other part comes from how our minds are
programmed. We basically *learn* how to express our sex, and
we can learn to express it either in a healthy manner or in a
way that is distorted and ultimately damaging to our
humanity. I continue to marvel at how something as
beautiful and fulfilling as sex can become so murky and
debased. But that's true for all the beautiful things of life,
isn't it?

IS ADDICTION TO SEX POSSIBLE?

Several years ago, I recall reading a letter to one of the
syndicated "advice columns": I cannot repeat the exact

letter, but it read something like this:

> Please help! My husband started out with girlie maga-
> zines. Now he's renting porno VCR tapes. He spends
> more time with that stuff than he spends with me. I think
> he's obsessed with this garbage, which turns me off the
> more it turns him on. Is there such a thing as sexual
> addiction? Can anything be done about it?

In the published response, the columnist agreed that
there is such a thing as "sexual addiction" and that the
husband might well have it. She referred the letter writer to
"Sexaholics Anonymous" and recommended that she insist
that her husband seek help. (Sexaholics Anonymous is a
program for both sexes who recognize that their preoccupation with sex is self-destructive.)

Was the columnist right? Can sex really be "addicting" in
the strictest sense of the word? I believe it can, for several
reasons:

1. *Sex provides pleasure.* I can say this from personal
observation, but there is also research evidence to support
the idea. No doubt a part of this is the possible tranquilizing
effect of the hormones involved in sexual arousal. For
example, the level of testosterone (the male sex hormone
produced in the testes) rises when erotic stimulation occurs.
This produces a feeling of well-being.[1] Orgasmic culmina-
tion produces a further pleasurable response, although
many report that great pleasure is derived from the sexual
encounter even when no climax has occurred. Research
indicates that the experience of sexual pleasure is *both*
physiological and psychological. It involves both body
chemistry and a state of mind. With such profound pleasure
to be had, it's little wonder that sex can become an addicting
agent.

2. *Sex creates a cycle of creating and reducing tension.* Sexual

arousal, in other words, causes a rise in sexual tension. As arousal increases, a state of unrest is created that "craves" fulfillment. This is how the body is designed. Sexual intercourse or masturbation to climax then provides the "relief" which is even more profoundly tranquilizing because a state of heightened tension was created just before the climax.

It's like fasting before a big meal. You deprive yourself of food so as to increase the tension of hunger pangs. Then you satisfy the craving by binging. Whenever such a cycle of enhanced tension or appetite followed by a tension-relieving behavior occurs, the risk of addiction is strong.

3. *Sex stimulates excitement.* (Actually, this is part of the pleasure it affords.) Sexual arousal is a powerful stimulant. We don't fully understand the biochemistry of this arousal, but there is evidence of increased circulating adrenaline (heart rate and even blood pressure go up), triggering of the autonomic nervous system (skin conductance increases due to sweating), and release of a natural form of amphetamine.

I am sure that my male readers will have experienced, as I have, sleep-disturbed nights when you have been sexually aroused but did not have an outlet for this arousal. The body becomes fully alive and alert. The mind won't let you off the hook and allow slumber. Your heart pounds away while your sex hormones crave fulfillment.

Now this sort of stimulation is in many respects more profound than that provided by many of the minor stimulant drugs like the caffeine of coffee or "wake-up" pills. The fact that the chemical changes originate from within makes no difference to the body. We can just as easily become addicted to our own body chemistry as we can to Colombian cocaine. This fact is so obvious that I am amazed it is not given greater prominence in drug counseling circles.

Some sociologists call the idea of sexual addiction a myth and question whether we can really apply the notion of "addiction" to sexual compulsions. Sexual addicts themselves, however, are not waiting for the scientists to make up their minds as to what it should be called. In the mid-1970s, a recovering alcoholic began experimenting with the Twelve Steps used by AA and applied them to his own sexual addiction. This gave birth to Sex Addicts Anonymous and later Sexaholics Anonymous (the group the advice columnist mentioned)—groups that are helping thousands of people to overcome their sexual addictions.

Sexual addictions can fall into several different categories. Lustful addictions (addictions to excessive sexual desire) are one form. Addictions to love and relationships are another. Perversions (addictions to distorted sexual practices) are yet another.

Sexual addictions can affect both males and females, although as a rule men and women seem to "prefer" different addictions. On the whole, males tend to be more prone to lustful addictions and females more likely to develop addictions to love and romance.

There is no question that males and females differ in both the biology and expression of sexuality.[2] Girls develop faster than boys, but males end up with greater physical strength. Females have greater tactile sensitivity and manual dexterity. Because males tend to be more aggressive (this may be more sociological than physical in its cause) and females more nurturing (they are the childbearers), differences in sexuality are bound to emerge. Males seem to need physical sex more than females, and females seem to need emotional sex or love more than males. Again, this may be purely cultural, and there are certainly many exceptions to this generalization, but my own observation of patients and friends supports this general statement. Males, for instance, seem to complain more about not getting enough sex than females but increasingly I hear similar complaints from my female patients. I also happen to believe that males tend to be more neurotic in their expression of sexuality than females; they seek to pervert sex more often.

This phenomenon of perversion complicates and exacerbates the problems of sexual addiction. By perversion, I simply mean sexual experience that deviates from the "normal." I know that "normal" can be very relative. It ought not to take a great intellect or a Kinsey-like survey to tell us what ought to be the proper and healthy way to express sexuality—but we certainly do struggle as a culture to find a balance here. Most, if not all, perversions are in my opinion variants of sexual addiction, so as we explore perverted sex, I hope we will develop a clearer understanding of what normal sex is all about. It is not the part of behavior you can define with ten do's and don'ts.

There are three kinds of sexual addiction, therefore, that I propose to cover in this chapter on sexual addictions: lust, romantic love, and perversion. Before I can move into these topics, however, I want to examine both our God-given capacity for sex and the way "neurotic" or "false" guilt can be a barrier to God's power to help us.

THE NEED FOR A THEOLOGY OF SEX

I am convinced that we desperately need a "theology of sex" in our churches today. I don't mean stricter moral rules. What we need is a balanced understanding of what God intends for us in this area of our lives.

Just how big a problem sex is for many Christians is shown by the volume of mail I receive on the subject. I receive many letters from readers of my books. (This is one of the great joys of being a writer—books can travel to the four corners of the world more effectively than any person.) Because I often speak to ministerial groups, I also get letters from pastors about their personal struggles. And a great many of these involve sex.

Rather than break confidence by quoting any one pastor's letter, let me present a composite of several letters which gives a very accurate picture of the personal feelings of *many* ministers and devout Christian men:

Dear Dr. Hart:
I am writing you this letter because I cannot tell anyone else about my feelings. People would think I was a total hypocrite if they knew what I have to deal with. My problem is sex. Almost every day of my life I feel strong sexual urges that threaten to overwhelm me. I have a loving wife, and she responds willingly to my sexual advances—but it never seems to be enough.

I feel very ashamed that I always look upon other women as sexual objects. Even though I am committed to treating all women with respect, I battle to keep my sexuality chained within myself. I have always masturbated—as long as I can remember. At first I used soft porn, but in recent years I can't resist the hard-core stuff. My sexual drive sometimes is so hard to control that I start thinking of it as an evil itself.

God knows how often I have prayed for deliverance. At times, when I am preoccupied with a challenging task, the flames seem to die down, but I always know these short periods will never last. A sensuous picture or a friendly glance from someone I admire just sends me into a frenzy again.

I don't think I'm the only one with this problem—in fact I know I'm not. The few fellow pastors I have shared my feelings with seem to struggle just as I do. I've studied all the books on temptation and know the verbiage and ten-point lists of advice—"Just stop thinking about sex," they say—but that's easier said than done. My only hope lies in the anticipation that as I get older the fire will slowly subside.

I present this letter to show that even the best among us must struggle with this, the most powerful of forces. The truth is that we are all tempted sexually and must constantly do battle with our hormones. This is not to say we cannot gain victory over our sexual urges. But such victory begins by facing the struggle honestly and admitting our deepest feelings.

There are two factors in our Christian subculture that contribute to the development of sexual addictions. The first is the reluctance (at least among males) to own up to and talk about our sexual urges and struggles. This reinforces denial, a major factor in addiction. The second factor is the breeding of guilt feelings.

The greater our burden of guilt, the stronger will be our urges in the realm of sexuality. (Obsessions and compulsions, for instance, are often an attempt to resolve deep-seated guilt feelings.) Conversely, the stronger our urges, the greater our feelings of guilt. The result is an addictive cycle that is very difficult to break.

What feeds the high incidence of guilt feelings we find in Christian circles?

1. *We are invested in a holy calling.* Pastor or layperson, we long to be holy and to follow Christ's example of purity and faithfulness to the Father. Driven by an unrelenting force of hormones, we then find ourselves focusing all our thoughts, behavior, and energy on sex, and this seems to be at variance with God's standards.[3]

2. *We are expected to have impeccable moral character.* Others expect it of us, and we expect it of ourselves. I don't think I have ever met anyone who can honestly say, "I live up to the expectations I have of myself." We all feel a little hypocritical. Some of us feel a lot hypocritical.

3. *We feel we are called to help other people solve their sexual temptations, but we are tempted ourselves.* We believe that physicians should first "heal themselves." But if most of us had to wait until we had resolved all our sexual struggles, we would never be able to help anyone at all. Fortunately, God calls sinners to minister to sinners.

4. *We have been taught to feel guilty about everything.* The feeling of guilt is a major dynamic in neuroticism. It is also easily distorted by faulty teaching. If an excessive, rigid, and tyrannical conscience is created very early in life, it has great difficulty ever responding to forgiveness. Instead, it demands punishment.[4]

Given the preponderance of *guilt feelings* (as opposed to true guilt) in our Christian world, it is not at all surprising to find a high incidence of obsessional sexuality—people feeling that they cannot control their sexual feelings. The foundation for this guilt is to be found in early childhood, where all neurotic or false guilt is created.

By "false guilt" I mean an excessive urge for self-punishment that feeds the addictive process. This kind of guilt is not "false" in the sense that one is not sinning. It is false because one cannot or will not receive forgiveness for the sin.

It is at this point that conviction by the Holy Spirit differs from conscience. While we may or may not feel guilty when God convicts us, he creates a state of *true guilt* in which we became aware of the nature of the violation—from God's perspective. This prompts us to repent, confess, change our ways, and receive forgiveness. True guilt, then, is designed for our healing.

False guilt, on the other hand, is unhealthy. It wants to wallow in self-pity, engages in persistent confession with no real desire for forgiveness, and flagellates self-esteem. What makes false guilt different from true guilt is it doesn't want to be forgiven; it doesn't want to change. Rather than accepting grace, it demands that we pay for our sins. And we do pay—through depression, emotional pain, and addiction to the very sin we are trying to avoid.

To illustrate, let me tell you Jon's story. Several weeks ago he came to see me about a persistent problem with depression. At twenty-four years of age, he has not yet "settled down." He is single and still living at home. He is also a Christian, very active in church affairs.

Jon's depression problem started, he told me, at about the time he became a Christian at age nineteen. At fairly regular intervals he becomes self-pitying, sad, despondent, and despairing. He thinks about taking his life. "God must hate me," he wails. "I let him down all the time. I'm unhappy and feel like a total failure."

When I pushed him as to why he was depressed at that moment, he finally broke down and told me about a sexual encounter he had the past weekend. He is attracted to a girl at his church, and she likes him. They decided to go to a movie together on Saturday evening. After the movie they went back to her apartment, and despite his determination not to get involved sexually, he couldn't resist her advances.

Now he feels terrible. Once again he has failed God. "I don't deserve God's love—I think I'll just throw in the towel."

As we explored Jon's guilt feelings it became clear that his guilt had a large neurotic component. He *felt* guilty but had no desire to repent—deep down, he did not want to give up his sexual behavior. God was trying to deal with him, but his childish, self-pitying reaction kept God out. As long as he wallows in his guilt and refuses forgiveness, his lust will remain a part of his life.

We have now begun to work on Jon's false guilt. He is beginning to understand why he does what he does and is starting to see some light at the end of the tunnel. Soon, I pray, God will break through his veneer of moralism and plant the seed of true righteousness.

A CHRISTIAN UNDERSTANDING OF SEX

Christians have not been excluded from the impact of the sexual revolution of the 1960s and 1970s. Its effect has been twofold. On the one hand, we seem to have lost any real ethical sense about sexuality. We don't know what is right anymore, and this creates serious problems for the future. At the same time, it seems that we have intensified our neurotic preoccupation with sex, creating an obsessional preoccupation with a need for extraordinary sexual excitement that is ravaging the emotions of pastors, Christian leaders, and laypersons. While you burn with passion, it is difficult to obey the call of Christ with a clear conscience.

What can be done about this problem? Is there a "theology of sex" that is relevant for today?

Christianity Today made an excellent beginning in a review of sexual mores entitled, "Great Sex: Reclaiming a Christian Sexual Ethic."[5] This article points out that the evangelical community has responded to the sexual revolution by trying to divorce a person's sexuality from his or her personhood. This is not biblical. Sexuality is basic to our sense of self—our understanding that we are God's creation. The secular world may see sex as a "thing" or an "activity," but a Christian sexual ethic views it as an integral part of life with God. Sexuality is essentially our way of living before God as male and female.

Building on that foundation, here are some additional thoughts to help us straighten out our view of sex and lower our propensity for sexual addictions:

1. *We must always aim at spiritual and psychological health.* We are called to renew our minds. But it is fruitless to attempt this renewing only from a human point of view. It is a product of the transformation God works in us (Rom 12:2).

2. *We must understand that God's creation is reflected within our bodies in sexual differences, and this is separate from the Fall.* Sex is not sin. It is how we express our sexuality that determines whether or not it is sinful. God created sex to be part of our lives (Gn 1:28). We should rejoice in it.

3. *We need to be on guard against distorting sex and turning it into a frenzied search for the "ultimate" pleasure.* Because it has been

contaminated by sin, sex has the potential to become distorted. In fact, because sex presents such compelling rewards, it has the greatest potential of all the human emotions to become distorted.

4. *We must strive for purity not because we feel guilty, but because following God's commands brings us closer to him.* François Mauriac once pointed out that most arguments for purity tend to be *negative arguments:* Be pure, or you will feel guilty.[6] But God commands purity for a *positive reason:* "Blessed are the pure in heart: for they shall see God" (Mt 5:8).

5. *We need total healing, not just healing of our sexual distortions.* Our sexual sins are just as much a reflection of our neuroticisms as they are a violation of God's laws. As such, they are impediments to our spiritual and emotional growth. We are the ones who suffer if we violate God's plan for our sexuality; we forfeit the growth of our character.

6. *We need to ensure that our repentance does not become a form of self-punishment.* God demands repentance as a condition of forgiveness; we tend to turn it into punishment. Herein lies a "catch-22" situation. If we use repentance for self-rejection and self-condemnation, we set up a barrier to God's forgiveness. Repentance is the doorway back to God, not a gauntlet of self-flagellation we must run in order to get back to God.

7. *We need to proclaim constantly that the power of God is greater than our sin and that his resources far exceed our most pitiful needs.* For many, these resources never get a chance because of the barriers I have been discussing. Preachers, teachers, and people-helpers need to apply greater wisdom to help people tap into these resources. Too often, I am sorry to say, the preaching I hear from our evangelical pulpits tends to set up barriers between people and God's resources, creating false guilt that resists grace—and this is especially true in the area of sexuality. Such preaching may help keep people dependent on the church, but it never turns them free.

LUST AS AN ADDICTION

Lust is sometimes called an "animal urge." Actually, however, it's uniquely human; it has its origins in the distinctive way the human brain is organized. In lower forms of life, sex is purely an instinctual urge. It is triggered by odors and carried out by reflexes. I very much doubt if a male dog can tell if another dog is male or female simply from outward appearance. Differences are communicated through scent—often pungent to the species but imperceptible to others.

In human beings, however, these functions are "moved up" higher in the brain; this transfer is known as "encephalization of function." The human sexual drive operates out of the "cortex," that thin outer layer of the brain where all learning takes place. Humans use their highly developed brains to *learn* how, when, where, and whether they will give expression to their sexual urges.

We are, therefore, not as instinctually driven as animals when it comes to sex. This makes us responsible for what we do and gives us the power to make choices. In other words, we are *more* than our hormones. We even have the ability, should we so choose, to suppress our sexual urges through the control that the cortex of the brain allows us to exert. This makes celibacy possible.

The fact that our sex drive is controlled by our brains also means that we can take the basic hormonally determined sex drive and *add power to it* with fantasy, thoughts, and preferences. And the more we "enhance" sex in this way, the more addictive it can become.

It is this brainpower, with its fantastic ability to symbolize and create "substitutes" for different objects, that turns visual objects into sexual objects. Pictures, for instance, can become charged with sexual significance even though they are just printed dots on a sheet of paper. For males, the sight of female breasts takes on special significance that goes beyond the breasts' created function to provide nurturing milk for babies (no other form of animal life regards the breasts as sexual symbols this way). Shapely legs or a particular waistline can also become symbolized and take on stimulating properties that get the sex hormones going. For the female, masculine builds or a particular ruggedness might do the same—though women tend to respond to visual cues less than men do.

This "symbolizing" of certain body parts that turns them into sexual objects is the beginning of the fetish phenomenon seen in most perversions. Remember, a fetish is an object that becomes a substitute object of devotion. A sexual fetish is a sexual symbol that substitutes for the real thing. For instance, a shoe or a stocking can come to be sexually significant in its own right.

Now here is the rub: The more we conceal parts of the body, the more we tend to create these fetishes. This concealment is, to some extent, necessary in modern society. Nevertheless, it is out of this "covering" of the human body that originated in the Fall that much sexual addiction arises.

Once we have created sexual "symbols," they seem to be permanently embedded in our minds. Fortunately, in a healthy person the brain can learn to separate symbols and sort them out, to "decide" when it is appropriate to become stimulated. This explains why a male gynecologist can clinically examine female sexual organs all day long without any sexual reaction and yet gets aroused when he goes home and sees his wife's peekaboo blouse.

Lust, therefore, is much *more* than just an animal drive. No animal spends its life fixating on sex; its sexual drive lasts only as long as the scent is in the air. Human beings are different; a large part of our sexuality is in our minds. Sexual health and harmony don't come from nature, therefore, but from the responsible exercise of appropriate choices. On the negative side, sexual addiction involves the participating of the mind in interpreting and directing the body's response to sexual stimulation.

An anonymous pastor, describing how he tried to analyze lust and "to fractionate it down into its particulars,"[7] provides a helpful analogy. He describes how it is possible to take a *Playboy* centerfold and study it with a magnifying glass. All he sees are dots—three primary colors and black— laid down by the printing press. There is no magic on the page, only tiny blobs of ink. Under magnification they show flaws and blurs. Still, when he pulls back, there is a sexual stimulus on that page. His blood steams when he gazes at it, and his sex drive takes over. Lust is a powerful force because it has the whole brain at its disposal, not just a few sex hormones.

Lust, then, is basically no more than the desire to experience the pleasure of sexual feelings. Up to a point it is normal, especially when focused on the right object, say a spouse. However, when it becomes addictive, it becomes unquenchable. Sex itself doesn't bring satisfaction; it creates tension—it stirs things up. The result is a vicious cycle of wanting what you can't have, feeling guilty about wanting it, feeling increased tension, and therefore craving more of what you can't have. It can drive many crazy.

How can we prevent lust from becoming an addiction? How can we honestly admit our desires and simply walk away from them before they run away with us? Here are some suggestions:

1. *Don't confuse lust with simple "attraction" or "admiration."* If you do, you will feed your false guilt and set a trap for yourself. It is quite natural to notice someone attractive and admire that person. One would have to be awfully "out of touch" with reality not to be able to notice attractiveness. There is much more to lust than admiration, however. The Greek word translated as "lust" is a broad word that literally means "strong desire." The Tenth Commandment, "You shall not covet your neighbor's wife," gets closer to the

issue. Unhealthy lust is not just admiring; it is "coveting"—being obsessed with acquiring something you don't have. Admiration recognizes what it sees—then walks away. It sets limits on what you desire.

2. *Don't focus on that which you find sexually attractive in someone of the opposite sex.* If you happen to look—and you will—don't linger. Accept and admit that what you see (or hear, or smell) is attractive, but don't continue thinking about it. Cut off your thoughts quickly and recognize the limits of what you can and can't have. Don't wallow in false guilt; obsession plays a major role in lustful addiction, and guilt is a major cause of obsession. Just accept your feelings, with God's forgiveness, and turn your thoughts and feelings away.

3. *Don't fantasize.* Sexual fantasies feed your brain with unwholesome images. Sexual fantasies that are intentionally created are clearly in the realm of lust. Often, of course, our fantasies catch us off guard; we can't help having them. Like dreams, they are not always consciously instigated. But the moment we become aware of them, we should turn away and reduce their power to stimulate us when it is inappropriate.

I see no value in sexual fantasies—not even to stimulate marital sex. It both causes and feeds wrong desires and sets up an expectation for ever-increasing excitement. Fantasies, especially about real people, demeans them. It robs them of their personhood. You have no right to use them this way.

4. *Set boundaries on the need to create novelty in sex.* Sexual satisfaction is often heightened by new places, positions, and other novelties. Occasionally, a married couple may enjoy an excursion to a hotel to get away from the kids, or a vacation alone for privacy. This helps to enhance the marital relations by allowing the couple to recapture some romance. But sex, like so many aspects of life, is subject to "tolerance" build-up. After a while, we habituate to one level of excitement and want more. Because of the very nature of

tolerance, however, there is no ultimate point at which you can be satisfied so do not overdo your quest for novelty.

5. *Bring masturbation under control.* This is a controversial topic, but one that affects many Christians. In my practice I am seeing more and more men who are caught up in masturbation, even though they are happily married. This is also true for women. Sometimes they claim their wives (or husbands) are unresponsive—but not always. The long wait between reaching puberty and getting married sets a trap for all of us and the only outlet for sex (short of engaging in premarital sex) is masturbation. Masturbatory practices, therefore, through this long waiting period can produce some major addiction tendencies in that they feed fantasy dependence and a quest for ever-increasing excitement.

I am not here to say whether masturbation is or isn't sinful. This matter is widely debated, with thoughtful and committed Christians on both sides. Whether simple masturbation for sexual release (without pornography or fantasy) is sinful or not is a matter for your personal conscience.

When masturbation becomes compulsive, however, it clearly *is* damaging. Compulsive masturbation invariably goes along with an obsession with pornography; it begins with excessive exposure to pornography while masturbating, normally in the early teens. Once this appetite has been created it is difficult to break—even when healthy marital sex is available. It easily becomes an addiction. I once heard a pastor describe the onset of his addiction in the following general terms:

Often I would find my father's *Playboy* magazine when my parents were out and pore over it, masturbating several times. Part of the excitement was the thrill of doing something wrong—misbehaving. This made for a higher climax. For the next five years I feasted on these magazines. Today, at thirty-five years of age, it is a constant struggle not to do the same.

6. *If your lust is obsessional or out of control, seek professional help from a competent Christian psychologist or counselor.* Your problem might be deeper than you realize and have its roots in a very repressive upbringing. God works through Christian psychotherapy as much as he does through other means of grace. He knows how troubled our brains can become when exposed to the wrong influences. He also knows what it takes to bring healing.

ADDICTION TO LOVE AND ROMANCE

Can love and a desire for romance also be addicting? I believe so. If problems with lust is predominantly a male issue, then addiction to relational love and romance is more often a female problem, it seems to me—although there is a lot of crossover. On the whole, the male seems more easily addicted to sexual novelty while the female is addicted to intimacy and attachment. Certain types of relationships are particularly addictive—at least that is what we are being told in popular magazine articles and books on how not to love too much.

Marie is a case in point. She never really knew her father. He left home and ran off with another woman when she was three years old and never bothered to contact her while she was growing up. Marie never consciously felt any desire to have any contact with him, either, until she turned seventeen. Then something happened to her feelings. She became obsessed with older men.

She sought them out, preferring their company over that of younger men. While she didn't particularly feel sexually attracted to them, she gave herself promiscuously in order to win their attention and affection. By the time she was twenty-one, she had had eight or ten affairs—usually with married men, always with men more than twice her age.

As we explored the reasons for this, Marie was able to identify the following sexual "forces" at work in her:

- She always longed for male closeness—the touch and hug of a man. Clearly, she longed for a father's love that she had never had.
- She realized she confused sexual arousal with deep love feelings. "When you want love—does it always have to go with sex?" she asked.
- She realized that no matter how many older men she fell in love with, nothing could fill the space that had been left by her missing father.

Finally, Marie realized she had become "addicted" to having affairs with older men because of her search for her long-lost father. A strange "transference" had taken place: she was transferring the love intended for him onto all men who were about his age. Upon realizing this, she quickly shut down the addiction, separated out her need for contact with her father from her need for a life-partner, and set that search in process. The healing process had now begun. She began to search for a relationship with someone nearer her age. She still has a long way to go, but a clearer understanding of why she sought affairs with older men helped her in making important choices about who she would or would not date.

We can identify several factors, then, that can lead to unhealthy, addictive love relationships:

- a search to fulfill a deep, unmet need,
- a belief that one can only be a "whole" or completed person when one is attached to another in romantic love,

- a desire to "lose oneself" and find identity through another,
- an irrational belief that connection with a partner will resolve all anxieties and neuroses and forestall all traumas,
- a determination to prove to oneself that one is worthy (sexually normal and exciting) by giving oneself to another.

Single adults are particularly prone to developing love and romance addictions. To those who have lived alone for a long time, the craving to be permanently united can become obsessional. To be deprived of sexual privileges is one thing; to be denied intimacy is far more devastating. Of course, many single people—divorced, widowed, and never married—find compensation in other friendships and live happy and well-adjusted lives. Some, however, fall prey to their exaggerated needs and wake up to find themselves in unhealthy relationships which may, in some cases, be the beginning of an addiction.

Married men and women can also fall prey to an addiction to romantic liaisons, especially later in life. Finding themselves bored and the marital bed devoid of excitement in the middle years, they often begin to fantasize—and then engage in illicit affairs. And I'm not necessarily talking about "worldly" people, either; this happens in the most spiritual of circles. Fatal attractions can easily take root anywhere, if given a chance. Fortunately, many fizzle out after a brief period, but some do not. Every church has its roster of "fallen" members and every denomination its list of fallen pastors who gave up all they had built up in the early years of marriage for the excitement of a midlife fling.

Now, we certainly cannot label everyone who has an affair as an addict. But for a number of these people, affairs become a habit and possibly an addiction. The addiction lies in the forces *beneath* the affair—the strong need for intimacy, the search for novelty in sexual expression, and the transference of many unresolved neurotic needs onto someone who is now being "idealized." Love stories as portrayed in novels, in the movies, and on TV don't help the problem, of course; often, this is where they get the idea.

Where does help lie for addictions to love and romance?

1. *We need to educate ourselves about the true nature of love and to strip it of the unrealistic glitter that Hollywood has painted on it.* Love is work—not fireworks. Love is commitment—not caressing. Love is giving—not getting.

2. *We need to clarify the true nature of romantic love.* There is a healthy romantic love (more like a very deep friendship with intimacy) and an unhealthy romantic love (fantasy-laden infatuation). The one is spiritual in nature, the other an addiction. The state we often call being "in love" is very much like an addiction; it is full of neurotic projection of unmet needs.

3. *If we are married, we need to focus on our marriage relationship.* Since our relationship with our spouse is to be our sole sexual focus, this is where we need to direct our attention. Building a good marriage is hard work. Every marriage begins with the union of two incompatible people in an impossible relationship. The task God gives us in marriage is to turn it into something beautiful. With God's grace—it *can* be done. I know, I've done it. After thirty-five years of marriage, I think I may be getting it right at last!

SEXUAL PERVERSIONS AS ADDICTIONS

I've left this topic until last because it covers the most serious of all the sexual addictions. *Psychology Today* estimates that there are about ten million compulsive sexual addicts in the United States.[8] These are people with serious personality disorders who have an addiction to some perverse aspect of sex as serious and destructive as any chemical dependency.

Living in Los Angeles, as I have for more than eighteen years, has made me very conscious of how perverse sex can become. We were recently made very aware of the "night-stalker" case, a serial killer who was convicted of murdering thirteen people, mostly women, many of whom were raped in the process. The connecting of murder with sex is the most bizarre of all perversions, and more common than we realize. Almost every city has its serial killers who stalk prostitutes in order to kill them in the act of sex. My reason for mentioning it here is to make the point that even these extreme perversions have the same underlying dynamics as the lesser ones.

Earlier in this chapter I described how it is possible to "add" other forms of excitement to our basic sexual pleasure. This is what happens with most perversions. When we experience sexual arousal with, say, fear, the two become linked in our minds, and the fear arousal adds to the sexual excitement. The ultimate kind of perversion, of course, is the linking of sex with pain or even death. This is the basis of sadomasochistic forms of sexual activity, in which pain is either given or received while being sexually stimulated.

For instance, there has been a marked rise in some cities of "scarfing" among younger people. It is estimated that between five hundred and a thousand adolescent boys and men accidentally hang themselves while scarfing every year.[9] This practice is technically known as "autoerotic asphyxia" and gets its name from the practice of tying ropes or "scarves" around the neck while masturbating, supposedly intensifying orgasm by cutting off oxygen to the brain. Scarfing kills when the victim accidentally slumps forward and strangles himself.

Experts are divided on what motivates people to take

such risks. Those who die seem intelligent, socially successful, and even do well in school. What they have in common is the tendency to be impulsive—risk takers. It is clear to me that this form of perversion has its cause in this incessant desire to "get more out of sex" that pervades our culture.

But lest we think of sexual perversion only in terms of serial killers or scarfers, let me hasten to add that "lesser" perversions dominate even our Christian bedrooms, often passing as respectable and normal. They are rationalized by ideas such as "As long as it enhances our marriage, it's OK," or "I can see no harm in our doing this." Participants are totally oblivious to how their "kinky" practices, usually driven by the need for ever-increasing excitement, can ultimately undermine the normal experience of sex.

THE ORIGIN OF SEXUAL ADDICTION

The most significant and pervasive expression of perversion we are faced with today is pornography. I have already discussed the obsessive and compulsive form of masturbation using pornography as a stimulus to excitement that is so prevalent among males. Here I want to talk about its origin. Where does it come from? What accounts for its prevalence in our culture? Usually it has its roots in a repressive environment with strong taboos against all forms of sexual expression.

I once counseled with a father (a prominent pastor) who had discovered that his sixteen-year-old son had a collection of hardcore pornographic magazines stored in a suitcase in his cupboard. One day the boy's mother had discovered it and in a panic told the father. He was beside himself. The mother tried to placate him: "He's a normal boy. Kids go through this stage. If you overreact you'll only make matters worse."

Up to a point she was correct. But what does a parent do in these circumstances? Do you condone your son's behavior? Do you ignore it? Or do you start World War III?

At root we must accept that this boy's problem is a reflection of the way sin and our society has distorted sex. It is not seen to be a normal expression of our humanity and procreation. We embellish it with mystique. We do not educate our children in a healthy understanding of its function. We forbid exposure of certain parts of the body from an early age, thus creating erotic curiosity. We don't talk about sex openly in Christian circles, let alone in our Christian families.

Add to this a repressive childhood environment (often caused by overly-rigid parents) and you have the fertile soil that creates a hunger for pornography, especially in males. Curiosity begins a process that may end in addiction. One devout Christian man told me:

> My mother kept drumming into me how terrible it was to notice girls or give any attention to the physical aspects of girls. This attitude kept me from facing my feelings. I was taught that the "physical" was wrong. Now I'm beginning to understand how pornography played a role in my later compulsions. Because I couldn't talk about my urges I became more preoccupied with them. I saw a nude magazine at a friend's house. I was overpowered by it. I couldn't believe that a woman would actually take her clothes off and be photographed. But I was hooked—and curiosity led to arousal and finally to addiction. All this time I cursed my father because he never discussed the wholesome aspects of sex with me.

This really is the bottom line, isn't it? In our culture it is very difficult to communicate to our children the "wholesome" aspects of sex when their desires for it start very young and legitimate fulfillment must be delayed until marriage. Teaching them how beautiful it is when confined to love in a marriage is necessary, but hard. Being open to hearing them talk about their struggles with sexuality is threatening, but necessary. I have *seldom* encountered a sexual addict who had open communication with healthy parents about sex while growing up. This says something, doesn't it?

I needed to emphasize the importance of healthy sex education in the home, but my main focus here is not so much on the preventive aspects but on the process of healing an addiction that has already set in. In addition to the general guidelines I will present in chapter twelve there are some important points to be borne in mind. I will begin with comments about the more serious addictions that may be damaging to others.

1. As with all healing in the realm of the emotions, the process begins with an honest acknowledgment of the problem. It is very easy to self-rationalize sexual addictions, whether the addiction is to pornography or some distorted expression of sexuality. Most extreme cases have to be confronted by loving friends or family because the addict refuses to see it as a distortion. This is especially true of those who engage in child sexual abuse (where there is often an addiction to the stimulation of the molestation). Sometimes it is even necessary to invoke legal proceedings to force the addict to face up to his or her problem. I only pray that if anyone reading this is engaging in child sexual molestation, they will seek help, even if they don't feel the need for it. Set aside your feelings and *do* what is right.

2. Whatever form of treatment you may seek from a professional, make sure you set up a system of accountability with at least one other person. Join a support group such as Sexaholics Anonymous or make a pact with a close friend to share all your feelings and to "report" to this person whenever you experience that your urges are out of control. Professional therapists can't always provide this

support. YOU CANNOT COPE WITH THESE POWERFUL URGES ALONE. This is especially true if a true addiction has set in.

3. For those whose addictions are not so serious in that they do not harm anyone else, I would also advocate joining a support group. I have treated several men with addictions to unusual sexual practices and in every instance the value of their being able to share their struggles with others (without necessarily revealing intimate details) has been greatly appreciated later. Usually it was with a Bible study or prayer group that also encouraged sharing. While I could explore the psychological dynamics of their addictions and help set up intervention strategies, they needed reassurance from "ordinary" people that they were still valuable as persons and encouragement to continue their struggle to overcome their addiction.

4. An understanding of how excessive guilt feelings can feed and maintain sexual addictions is crucial to overcoming an addiction. Of course, there is a healthy guilt that accepts responsibility and motivates a desire to change. This is not what I am talking about. The guilt feelings that arise because we may have been taught as a child that to touch a private part is "sinful," or to peep at mommy or daddy when they are getting dressed is "evil" or to feel any strong sexual urge is enough to damn you to hell can be so entrenched (and unconscious) as to be incapacitating all your life. What amazes me is that even in these so-called sexually enlightened days parents still create these feelings in children.

This guilt must be addressed. It doesn't go away easily. This is the guilt that drives a person to masturbate to pornography. It is the guilt of doing something wrong (learned in childhood) that adds the excitement that feeds it as an addiction.

How do we resolve this guilt? It begins with a deep experience of God's forgiveness. When repentance is deep and genuine, God can work a miracle in the dark recesses of our childhood conditioning. But further steps are also necessary:

a. Accept your sexuality as a gift from God. Accept your feelings of sexuality as a part of your body's functioning. Don't resist it. Don't deny it. Don't spiritualize it in the sense of labeling it as sin.
b. Accept that control, self-control, is part of the price for being human. Just because you feel an urge for something doesn't mean you must experience it.
c. Avoid situations that stimulate your addictive urges. If you crave sexually explicit movies, choose not to go to them. If you crave a pornographic magazine, don't drive through the sleazy part of town where the shops are located. "Resist" these temptations. There is NO OTHER WAY. You must exercise your will to change. Every alcoholic knows that no one else can change you, only you can.

5. The ultimate solution for overcoming sexual addictions that do not directly harm others is to build a balanced life (the topic of part three of this book) and find a mature way of expressing the fullness of your sexual urges through marriage. If the sexual part of your marriage is not satisfying then the problem may be in your marriage or in yourself. Either way, you may benefit from going to talk the matter over with an understanding pastor or counselor. My only plea is: Don't put it off! Problems do not fix themselves. Years later you may regret not having attempted to find a solution earlier.

TEN

Addiction to Adrenaline: Hurry Sickness

B EHIND ALL THE MAJOR ADDICTIONS is a compelling urge to feel wonderful and avoid pain—physical or emotional. And one of the commonest ways we pursue this goal of exalted delight is through the use of the body's own natural and powerful stimulant—adrenaline.

I recently came across an advertisement for a new sports car. The photograph depicted a sleek, red, obviously power-ful dream car. Across the top of the ad were the words, "pure adrenaline." That just about sums up the attitude of most of us today, even if we don't know it! In our society we worship adrenaline and all it offers—increased vitality, delayed pain, and deep euphoria—to such an extent that I believe it is our greatest addiction problem.

What is adrenaline addiction? Just what the name implies: we become "hooked" on the pleasurable feelings produced by a group of adrenal hormones manufactured by the adrenal glands. Produced by the body and intended to produce "fight or flight" in an emergency situation, these hormones, known as catecholamines, are the body's stress hormones. And chief among them is adrenaline.

THE GOOD NEWS AND BAD NEWS
ABOUT ADRENALINE

Adrenaline and the other stress hormones play a vital role in helping us cope with emergency situations. When our life is threatened, when we are frightened or have to deal with a crisis, these substances come to our rescue. They give us extra energy, strength, and alertness. They enable us to perform feats of endurance and remarkable courage.

That's the *good* news.

The *bad* news is that people tend to *develop a lifestyle* that constantly recruits adrenaline; it's like living in a state of emergency. Under these conditions, adrenaline is destructive. It increases circulating cholesterol and fatty deposits in our arteries—putting us in danger of heart disease. It thickens the blood (so we can't bleed as easily in an emergency)—increasing the likelihood of an embolism. It engages the viscera so that gastric juices flow strongly— making us prone to ulcers and other problems of the digestive tract. It raises the blood pressure chronically, putting us at risk for stroke.

In a genuine emergency, then, adrenaline and its fellow stress hormones can preserve our lives. When abused or overused, they can kill us!

As I have shown in earlier chapters, these powerful hormones can also *addict* us. Many people find the "rush" that comes with surging adrenaline quite pleasurable and easily reach the point where they deliberately seek it out. The body soon adapts to this high level of arousal, just as it does to any stimulant drug. (The body knows no difference between external and internal chemistry.) With this adaptation comes the classic addictive need for more, along with its associated symptoms of denial and inability to control the dependence. A full-blown addiction develops, complete with tolerance effect and withdrawal symptoms. I will explore this process in more detail as we proceed through the chapter.

THE HURRIED PERSONALITY

Adrenaline is both the cause and consequence of what is commonly called "hurry sickness"—the plague of modern civilization. The connection between time urgency, elevated adrenaline, and stress-related disease is well established.[1] I am more convinced than ever that hurry sickness and its underlying abundance of adrenaline is an addiction as potent and ultimately as destructive as cocaine or alcohol.

Do you have hurry sickness? Try taking the test shown in table 5, "Are You Addicted to Hurry?" This test will help you see whether this common form of adrenaline addiction is a problem for you. It measures whether you are addicted to hurry or urgency.

TABLE 5

Are You Addicted to Hurry?

The following test measures whether you are addicted to hurry or urgency. Answer TRUE or FALSE to the following questions:

TRUE FALSE

___ ___ 1. Even though I have never done it, I think I would enjoy riding a motorcycle.

___ ___ 2. I get restless whenever I have nothing to do.

___ ___ 3. I frequently look at my watch or a clock nearby.

___ ___ 4. In conversations, I prefer to get right to the point rather than beat around the bush.

___ ___ 5. People who talk slowly irritate me.

___ ___ 6. I cannot sit still for very long.

TABLE 5 (*continued*)

TRUE FALSE

___ ___ 7. I often find myself finishing other people's sentences for them.

___ ___ 8. When I go on vacation, I prefer a place with lots of activity, not a quiet place.

___ ___ 9. I much prefer to use the express line in a supermarket.

___ ___ 10. Long delays at traffic signals irritate me.

___ ___ 11. I hate standing in line for anything.

___ ___ 12. I often have more tasks to do in a day than time to do them.

___ ___ 13. When I try to go to sleep, my mind often rehearses all the things I haven't been able to accomplish that day.

___ ___ 14. When I am delayed and arrive at an engagement late, I am irrationally upset because I can't stand being late for anything.

___ ___ 15. I have difficulty finding time for a haircut or even for a regular physical checkup.

_____ Total number of TRUE responses:

Scoring: The higher the number of TRUE responses, the more likely you are to be addicted to hurry. Your score can be interpreted as follows:

0 to 3: Normal hurriedness

4 to 7: Moderate tendency to be hurried; you could benefit from slowing down.

8 to 15: You are clearly addicted to hurry and urgently need to slow down.

Vern, a patient of mine, is clearly a "hurried personality." At home and the office, in church, or when engaging in his favorite form of recreation, bowling, Vern is in a tremendous rush. Although he is quite secure in his job as a financial manager for a large company, he always *feels* insecure enough to have to "push it." He hurries to the next meeting, grows impatient at the smallest sign of inefficiency, rushes through telephone calls, zips through budgets, and arranges the next round of meetings, all with a sense of urgency.

Vern describes himself to me with the words of the white rabbit in *Alice in Wonderland:* "I'm late! I'm late, for a very important date!" He doesn't seem to be able to slow down anymore; his rush has become a part of his personality. And he likes it that way. Being in a hurry makes him feel alive, important, efficient.

Underlying Vern's all-consuming need to complete tasks as quickly as possible, of course, is an overproduction of stress hormones, notably adrenaline. Vern has become addicted to the sense of excitement and stimulation this hormone provides. His life, therefore, has become a frenzied race to begin new tasks even before the old ones are completed.

Vern's obsession with time has distorted all his values. To him, wasting time is a sin—and anyone who "takes things easy" is lazy and immoral. This has led to much conflict with his teenage son, who is a more "laid back" type—mostly in reaction to his father's compulsion. He is easygoing— perhaps too much so. And he drives Vern up the wall.

But what is perhaps the most fascinating aspect of Vern's story (which in many respects is also my story) is how he reacts to *forced idleness.* When Vern is forced to slow down or take a vacation, he nearly goes berserk. This reaction to slowing down is, in my opinion, the clearest evidence that the excessive use of adrenaline is addicting—it's a very clear pattern of withdrawal symptoms. I myself have experienced a milder form of this reaction of lowered adrenaline.

What are some of the signs of adrenaline withdrawal?

- a strong compulsion to "do something,"
- an obsession with "what has been left undone,"
- a vague feeling of guilt,
- a mild to moderate feeling of depression (called "post-adrenaline depression"),
- fidgetiness, restlessness, pacing, leg kicking, finger drumming, or fast gum chewing,
- feelings of irritability and aggravation.

The experience of "postadrenaline depression" is very common and an important symptom. Often it is felt on weekends or after a period of intense activity. Pastors feel it on Mondays, and sports enthusiasts (players and spectators) experience it the day after the big event. The depression is caused by the steep drop in the level of adrenaline and is part of the restorative process of the body.

Because the symptoms of adrenaline withdrawal are unpleasant, most people tend to react to them by stepping up the supply of the "drug." We "psych ourselves up" and return to the pressure cooker as fast as possible. Not only does this accelerate normal "wear and tear" of our bodies, thus hastening the onset of stress and heart disease, but it produces many *distress signals* in the body: ulcers, headaches, and gastric distress, to name but a few.

Withdrawal following periods of high activity, then, along with the urge to return to that activity, is a major indication of adrenaline addiction. There are other indications as well. The signs of adrenaline addiction can be summed up as follows:

- evidence of "withdrawal" symptoms during periods of forced idleness or lowered adrenaline demand,
- periodic mild depressions, usually following a period of intense stress or high challenge,
- increased proneness to anxiety, with a tendency to panic or a feeling of flight,
- increased tendency to obsess about things you have no control over and to engage in compulsive behaviors.

We will see as we proceed how these symptoms weave in and out of the pattern of adrenaline addiction.

ADRENALINE ADDICTION AND PLEASURE STIMULATION

Since most of my discussion here focuses on how an emergency hormone like adrenaline can become addicting, and because all addictions involve an experience of pleasure, let me comment briefly on how adrenaline addiction relates to *pleasure stimulation* and how spiritual factors (both good and bad) can create a need for pleasure.

A pastor in one of my classes recently reminded me of the similarity between the science fiction novel *The Terminal Man* and adrenaline addiction. In this novel, a man has electrodes placed deep within in his brain so that he can be stimulated to correct his antisocial behavior. (Remember, it is only a novel. I doubt if such stimulation actually cures antisocial behaviors.) The problem is that these stimulations turn out to be extremely pleasurable. The sensations he receives as he presses the switch and sends small electrical pulses through the electrodes is so enjoyable that he quickly becomes addicted to it. He demands more and more of it. He can't stop pressing the switch. The result is that he becomes a homicidal maniac when the researchers try to remove the switch.

Now this is "sci-fi," but it is not as far-fetched as it seems. Similar experiments have actually been conducted with rats. Such stimulation of the brain's pleasure center can be so pleasing that rats also are set up to administer the pulses themselves have been known to die of starvation by neglecting food rather than stop giving themselves their shots of ecstasy. Criminals, sky divers, workaholics, and lovers are not that far removed from this behavior. Their ecstasy can set up a strong craving for the behavior that produces the ecstasy. This is the very foundation of all addictions.[2]

Scientifically and psychologically we have now reached a turning point in *understanding* how pleasure is produced, but we still cannot *control* it to any satisfactory extent. This ought to tell us something about the limitations of knowledge! It's important to seek understanding, but understanding is not enough. We must use our understanding to connect us more effectively with the power God can give us to *control* our addictions.

Advances in our scientific understanding of the mechanisms of neurotransmission (the way the brain sends and receives signals) have led to a much greater appreciation of how the mind and the body interact. They operate in unity, not as two separate machines. We can change our brain chemistry through stimulating thoughts and activities just as easily as with drugs.

This leads some researchers to downplay the role of spiritual and moralistic factors in addiction.[3] I believe this is most unfortunate, because my personal experience and clinical work strongly demonstrate that pleasure seeking has powerful spiritual and moral aspects as well. Sin and the human predilection for disobedience cannot be ignored as mind-altering activities. This is underlined by the fact that most compulsive behaviors center around activities that are generally considered "wrong." Very few people develop a compulsion to be generous, for example. More often, it is when we believe something to be wrong that we feel compelled to do it more. This is why sin is attractive to us.

I don't believe that compulsive behavior is solely a creation of the brain and its fifty billion or so nerve cells. While biological interconnections (trillions of them) are made as we learn and lay down patterns for seeking pleasure, the basic drive for pleasure is psychological and spiritual as well. Adrenaline arousal is the chemical trigger for our heightened pleasurable sensations, and these sensations can become as addicting as alcohol.

I don't know to what extent spiritual factors can create a need for pleasure stimulation outside of body and mind operations. I do believe, however, that God generally works through our *total human framework* and that sin, while it may begin as a spiritual problem, finds its ultimate expression through hormones, muscles, and brain cells.

In other words, my desire to steal may begin as sin in my heart, but it has to be translated into a mental plan and body movements before it becomes sinful behavior. I think it is reasonable to assume, therefore, that our desires for pleasure may have large chunks of sin motivating them. The behavior that spurs our adrenaline to action may set up a primary chemical addiction, but the mind and the spirit are inseparably linked to this behavior.

This close connection between body, mind, and spirit is what the apostle Paul was getting at when he wrote:

> ... I am sold into slavery with Sin as my owner. I don't understand myself at all, for I really want to do what is right, but I can't. I do what I don't want to—what I hate.... It is sin inside me that is stronger than I am that makes me do these evil things. Rom 7:14-17 LB

Paul was talking about the rebellion that sin engenders, of course, but his description comes quite close to that of an addiction. It emphasizes that sin is not just immorality or disobedience to God's laws. It is a kind of bondage—a slavery, if you will. I believe it's reasonable to suggest that this slavery can involve being hooked on the quest for pleasure, including the exciting pleasure we derive from hormones like adrenaline. Why else does Satan focus mainly in the realm of our appetites when he tempts us? The great seducer knows how our adrenaline connections work. He needs to be resisted right at the point of our need for excitement and an adrenaline "fix."

BEYOND ADRENALINE ADDICTION—
ADRENALINE EXHAUSTION

Adrenaline addiction can be damaging enough in itself. Beyond adrenaline addiction, however, lies even more trouble—adrenaline exhaustion.

I had a friend some years ago who was hooked on skydiving. (You know what I mean—colorful parachutes and long delays before you pull the ripcord.) He was dating a young girl my wife and I both knew. Before long he got her interested, and both of them would spend their weekends looking for the ultimate thrill as they fell out of the sky. While they were by no means reckless and took every appropriate precaution, nevertheless they openly admitted that it was the risk element of the sport that attracted them; it gave them an adrenaline rush.

But skydiving was not the only adrenaline-recruiting pastime my friend engaged in. He loved daredevil rides in amusement parks and playing games like "chicken"; all these served to reinforce his underlying addiction to adrenaline.

Unfortunately, as with all addictive behaviors, my friend used his high-stimulation activities as a form of escape. As a consequence, he never really developed any sense of responsibility. He kept running away from obligations. Just two weeks before he was supposed to get married, in fact, he packed his things and went to sea, telling his fiancé that he would be back in six months—that he needed to get something "out of his system."

Unfortunately, the story did not end there. When my young friend did return he was found to be suffering from a profound state of adrenaline exhaustion.

You see, the adrenaline supply for the body is not unlimited. Sooner or later, if pushed to the limit by prolonged stimulation, the adrenal glands will "switch off," and a state of "hypoadrenia," or adrenaline fatigue, will set in.

My friend had all the symptoms. His lymph nodes had begun to shrink, severe fatigue had set in, a great weakness had come over him, he had lost weight, and he had become intensely nervous and fearful, experiencing symptoms similar to panic attacks. Many months of bed rest were required for his healing, during which he had to totally avoid all stimulation. He was paying the price for living on adrenaline too long.

Over the years I have seen several cases like this, in which it seems that the reserves of the adrenal glands become totally depleted. The syndrome can be recognized in its early stages by the following symptoms:

1. *The adrenaline addict suffers increased depressions of short duration, each resembling a major depression.*

2. *The addict finds it very difficult to get adrenaline going once it stops*—so he or she tries to avoid letting it down. Addicts in the early stages of adrenaline exhaustion don't sleep too long or rest too much.

3. *The addict increasingly suffers episodes of profound tiredness.* Most of us who are just "normal" adrenaline overproducers know this feeling from occasional periods of overwork; it comes not so much from physical exertion but from mental overactivity. Adrenaline addicts in the early stages of adrenaline exhaustion feel it at increasing intervals.

4. *The addict develops strange body sensations.* This is known as "parasthesias." The victim describes these feelings as strange sensations crawling up and down the arms or legs or profound itchings that won't go away when scratched. There may also be unexplainable pain. These "distortions" of body sensations can be extremely debilitating, disturbing sleep and causing much anxiety.

5. *Other stress symptoms, such as skipped or extra heartbeats, develop when the addict lies down to rest.* When the heart is overstimulated by adrenaline on a regular basis, all sorts of

irregularities are created. The addict feels them most when his or her adrenaline drops, and they can heighten anxiety tremendously.

6. *The addict may experience panic attacks.* During these periods of prolonged emergency response, natural brain tranquilizers are depleted. There is then an increased risk for the panic attacks that come with severe anxiety (see my book *Overcoming Anxiety*).[4] In fact, I don't think I have ever seen a case of severe panic disorder that did not also involve an overproduction of adrenaline—if not addiction.

COPING WITH ADRENALINE ADDICTION

Adrenaline cannot be ignored, and you can't live without it. Up to a point it is needed; beyond that point it becomes destructive. A major task in coping with it, therefore, is knowing where that point is. It's impossible to give any definitive guidelines; every individual is different. But if you suffer frequently from any of these traditional stress symptoms, it's a safe bet you are overadrenalized, probably because of stress or overstimulation:

- frequent headaches—tension and/or migraine,
- generalized panic and anxiety problems,
- elevated blood pressure with light-headedness,
- rapid heartbeat or skipped beats,
- general gastric distress—nausea, heartburn, diarrhea,
- general muscle pain,
- teeth grinding and jaw pain,
- feelings of trembling and fidgetiness, pacing,
- feelings of fatigue and general lack of energy,
- excessive sleep disruption.

Adrenaline addiction can be as resistant to change as any "hard drug." In some ways, it may be *more* resistant. The fact that it is socially acceptable, even admired in our success-driven culture, may make it even harder to "kick." Adrenaline addicts can't go "cold turkey"; all of us, even addicts, need the hormone for emergency situations. And adrenaline is always with us; our body's chemical factory goes wherever our bodies go. Imagine a heroin addict having to walk around with a package of "smack" in his back pocket!

Even if change isn't easy for the adrenaline addict, however, change is possible. Healing of adrenaline addiction involves three general areas of change:

- making changes in lifestyle,
- making changes in personality,
- developing the spiritual skills for inner peace and quietness.

Lifestyle Changes. Human beings need time for restoration and recovery. This human need for rest is a clear biblical concept. In the Bible, rest is not only a necessary part of the human life cycle; it is also linked with worship: "Six days thou shalt work, but on the seventh day thou shalt rest . . ." (Ex 34:21). The seventh day was to be a holy day, set apart for worship, no matter what was waiting to be done. This principle tends to be misunderstood and misused in Christian evangelical circles. We abuse our bodies for six days—then spend the seventh in religious activities that are as adrenally demanding as what we do during the other six days.

Rest is vital to our physical, mental, and spiritual health. In addition, without regular time set aside for rest and recovery, we cannot overcome adrenaline addiction. Adrenal glands become enlarged to meet the continual demand, and the self-destructive side effects continue unabated.

Here are some specific changes you need to make in your lifestyle:

1. *Don't try to rush your healing from adrenaline addiction.* If you

already suffer from hurry sickness, you will probably want to hurry your recovery as well. Remember, this attitude is part of the problem. Allow yourself space and time to make the necessary changes in your life. Work at learning patience, and try to keep your problems in perspective. Remember, it may have taken you ten, twenty, or even thirty years to get to where you are now. Don't expect any sudden changes—unless God works a miracle in your life. (Even then, he may choose to work a miracle that unfolds gradually rather than revealing itself all at once.)

2. *Accept responsibility for your problem.* Don't blame your parents. Don't blame yourself. Just accept responsibility to change. It is common for addicts to blame their job, their boss, society, their kids, their house—you name it—for their problems. Attaching blame is part of denial. So keep reminding yourself that your addiction is maintained not by the actions of these other parties, but by your reaction to them.

3. *Incorporate healthy physical changes.* Since adrenaline addiction is a physical as well as a psychological and spiritual phenomenon, certain skills and abilities that help the body manage adrenaline can help tremendously. Regular exercise, for instance, burns off excess adrenaline. Relaxation techniques can promote natural lowering of adrenaline. Getting enough sleep allows rejuvenation of the adrenal glands.[5]

4. *Beware of becoming obsessed with "time management" strategies.* Achievement-oriented go-getters (typical adrenaline addicts) tend to love managing their time to the nth degree. I believe this can be a pitfall.

It's not that I'm against time management. If you are disorganized and careless about schedules, learning to manage your time can do a lot to reduce stress in your life. My concern is that adrenaline addicts almost by definition tend to carry the efficiency philosophy to an extreme.

The goal of healthy time management is to create more

time to enjoy life and live for God. Adrenaline addicts tend to use the time they save through time management to engage in more tasks and thus create *more* stress!

At one point in my early adult years, I became very preoccupied with "efficiency." As a young engineer (my first profession) I became caught up with "time and motion" study. I remember reading *Cheaper by the Dozen* and the writings of the great developer of efficiency methods, Frank B. Gilbreth.[6] I tried doing more than one thing at a time—like shaving with one hand while applying antiperspirant with the other. I tried to plan every trip to be efficient. If I went to my bedroom, I asked myself, "What needs to be taken back?" Every trip needed to accomplish more than one purpose. I tried reading while walking, a habit that has stuck with me ever since. (It can be quite dangerous!)

Fortunately, the fad died a natural death; it was too much work. I've now learned, I hope, the importance of separating those areas of my life that need efficiency from those areas that just need "to be." I have come to appreciate the value of a slower pace and times for rest. This means I can now make the right choices about when to work and when to rest. I commend this separation to you also.

5. *Learn to tolerate frustration.* Accept that in the natural world projects will grind to a halt, people will let you down, and lines will get long just before you go to the checkout counter. In order to keep your adrenaline low, you have to learn to put up with interruptions and changes in plan. If you are adrenaline addicted, your body has learned that "fighting" is the appropriate response to every obstruction and challenge. So teach your body to calm down and accept the uneven flow of life without becoming angered. Controlling self-talk can be important here. Whenever you are frustrated at not getting your way, reassure yourself by saying, "This is not a perfect world and people are also imperfect. I must accept this and plan other ways to overcome my frustration."

6. *Learn to tolerate the slowness of others.* Adrenaline addicts move faster, think faster, talk faster, eat faster, shop faster, but die sooner than others. I know it can be very irritating to be slowed down by inefficiency, playfulness, or plain old cussedness! But I am slowly learning the value of taking things in stride and not working or driving near the speed limit.

7. *Use "disengagement" techniques.* These are techniques that put you into *neutral* gear—so that you are not being driven but coasting smoothly. These techniques can help you carry out the suggestions above:

- Catch yourself when you are in a hurry or racing from too much adrenaline.
- Apply the brakes, so to speak, and consciously slow down your action.
- Relax your mind and your body.
- Remind yourself of the futility of hurrying and the damage it can cause you.
- Schedule appointments, activities, meetings, and obligations to allow you a breather several times each day.
- Block out time for yourself at the beginning and end of each day.
- Use this "private time" for reflection, spiritual enrichment, perspective building, leisurely walking, or watching the sun rise or set.

8. *Reorder your values and make sure that your priorities, goals, commitments, and friendships are what you really want.* Stop trying to please others or keep up with them. Get off at the next station of your life's journey and take time to rearrange your priorities. There'll be another train along soon enough.

Personality Changes. Personality both causes adrenaline addiction and is shaped by it. We bring to adult life a set of traits that predispose us to getting hooked on hurry; our hurry then accentuates the traits it feeds on.

Your personality may have changed over the years as well. Maybe you don't have time for the good things of life anymore. You've forgotten how to relax or enjoy leisure. Your feelings may be out of control—too much anger and impatience. Perhaps your laughter has turned cynical; your good nature has become sarcastic. This is what adrenaline addiction can do to you. Right now you could probably do with a personality transplant!

Fortunately, however, God is in the business of changing people. Here are some ways you can facilitate this change:

1. *Prepare yourself for change.* Personality change can only take place if you are willing for it to happen. No one can force it on you.

2. *Make an inventory of personality traits you want to change.* Pray over this list and ask God to reveal to you *his priorities* for your changing.

3. *Accept the fact that change might be very slow.* Since personality traits, by their very nature, are enduring qualities, changing them takes time. It helps to focus on changing just *one* trait at a time. For instance, if you have become sarcastic in recent years, try changing this trait *only.* You are more likely to succeed this way. Once you have, you can move on to other traits.

4. *Increase your awareness of negative traits.* Ask your friends to help you in this—pointing out when you display the trait you're trying to change. Invite your spouse to do this, too—and try not to get defensive.

5. *Exercise choice at the point you become aware of negative traits.* Apologize if necessary and *choose to change.* In the past decades we have tended to downplay the role of free choice. We want to believe that some deep, dark, hidden force controls what we do. I used to believe this. Experience teaches me that this is not altogether true. We have a lot more control than we think.

6. *Depend on God for the power to change, but don't expect God to*

raise his hand and miraculously change your personality. It's not that God couldn't do it. But if he had wanted you to be an angel, he would have created you one to begin with. God is in the business of sanctification. He wants us to *collaborate* with his intentions, to use his power to help us grow, to create in us a living example of his purpose.

Develop Spiritual Skills for Inner Peace and Quietness. I will have more to say about this in the final chapter, but some reflection on how important it is to develop the spiritual skills for creating inner peace is appropriate here.

Abraham Lincoln reportedly once said, "The best thing about the future is that it comes only one day at a time." That sums up God's call to us about the way we live our lives: *We need to learn to live day to day.* God offers us peace— but *only* for today. If we want peace tomorrow, then we have to sow the seeds for it today and wait for the strength he will provide tomorrow.

Repeatedly I have stated that addictions arise when we are incapable of facing the reality of life. When tensions, problems, and anxiety become too overwhelming, we turn to some distraction and develop an addiction to it. Unfortunately, the escape from reality is only temporary—and we have the ugly reality of the addiction to deal with as well.

What, then, is the ultimate solution to the frightening anxieties that the realities of life create in us? It is an inner peace that only God can give—through Jesus Christ. He says:

"Peace I leave with you, my peace I give unto you: not as the world giveth, give I unto you. Let not your heart be troubled, neither let it be afraid." Jn 14:27

This legacy of peace has been claimed by countless people down through the ages. But what spiritual skills are needed to make it a reality for today? The quick and obvious answers are prayer, Scripture reading, witnessing to Christ's saving power, and so on. And these *are* important. But the problem with adrenaline addiction is that you can apply the same hasty motives to these spiritual disciplines that you do to your daily activities! For this reason I am convinced the *only* spiritual activities that are truly effective in creating inner peace are those that are undertaken *without* adrenaline.

This is not to say that God won't answer your hurried and hassled prayers. Fortunately, he always makes allowances for our failings. But prayer and spiritual disciplines *will not help you grow* in your inner spirit while you are still hooked on adrenaline.

The title of a classic book by Brother Lawrence[7] captures the essence of those skills we need to experience complete and abiding inner peace: we need to "practice the presence" of God. This involves:

- a total abandonment to God,
- a surrender of the priority of this life,
- an embracing of the priority of eternity,
- realizing that our sanctification does not depend on changing our works, but in doing for God what we ordinarily do for ourselves,
- bringing God into every action of every day,
- being in constant communion with God,
- being obedient to all his commands,
- regularly "retreating" from daily pressures to be available for God's communion with us.

We need to "practice his presence" not just intellectually, but with deep feeling, so that it becomes a regular habit. Then the constant benefit of God's presence can strengthen and restore us because it nurtures our spirit, nourishes our mind, cleanses our soul, and restores our balance. With these blessings, no addiction has a chance of surviving!

ELEVEN

Addictions to Food

O F ALL THE HIDDEN ADDICTIONS, addiction to food comes closest to the substance addictions. Binging on sugar-laden candies may have more in common with the overuse of pep pills than we realize. Swigging large amounts of caffeine-loaded coffee may not be that different from sniffing cocaine. The difference between food addictions and drug abuse may only be that the one is socially acceptable while the other isn't.

There are some differences, however. Many food addictions involve not only an actual substance but also an associated "process." Eating itself—the act of chewing, tasting, swallowing, and overfilling the belly—may have addictive elements that are quite separate from what is eaten. Food not only provides the body with a certain substance; it also provides the mind with a great degree of pleasure.

So our concern here must not only be with the *type* of food in which we indulge, but also with the *process of eating*. Either or both can be the basis for a hidden addiction.

It is hard to draw the line between food and eating. In a given addiction, how can we tell when the addiction is to food and when it is to eating? Perhaps it is always a bit of both. The pleasure and stimulation of food is felt well before it hits the stomach and digestion begins. The sight, smell, and taste of it can be highly pleasurable. The act of eating and even the enlargement of the stomach as it receives the food may all contribute some aspect of the addiction. The brain receives and processes many messages from all the senses associated with food, in order to control the whole process. As the executive center, it receives and transmits messages all the time to increase or decrease secretion of enzymes and acids, stomach movement, and production of bile. It is a very intricate operation.

We cannot detach the brain from our stomach. Therein lies the complex problem of food addiction.

THE MANY PURPOSES OF FOOD

Food serves many purposes, and each one has some ability to set up an addiction:

1. *Food nourishes and provides energy.* Those foods, therefore, that are high energy boosters (some can even be considered "turbochargers") can create a craving for this extra zest.

2. *Food gives pleasure to all the senses.* Within reason, this pleasure is normal and even necessary to good health; when food doesn't provide pleasure, we tend not to eat, and this can be physically debilitating. But as with all pleasure-producing substances and activities, the pleasure food gives can be used to relieve tension or disengage from reality—and the result is an addiction.

3. *Food pacifies.* I am quite convinced that food tranquilizes. What the mechanism for this is, I'm not sure. There may be more than one.

One possibility is that food, like sex, creates a tension-release cycle. Hunger sets up restlessness, tension, and irritability. Then, when we finally get to eat, the system is calmed. Part of the tranquilizing effect of food, therefore, is simply the "switching off" of the hunger rebellion. After all, food is essential to survival, so it makes sense that we were created to panic when food is cut off.

Another element of food's tranquilizing effect may come directly from certain foods that contain pacifying substances. (Milk, for instance, contains certain sleep-inducing chemicals.) Yet another factor may be the lethargy induced by an overfilled stomach. The desire to take a nap after a big lunch comes from this. The stomach needs so much blood to carry out its digestive functions that there isn't enough to keep the brain and the rest of the body working at top speed.

Having grown up in Africa, I am quite intrigued by the role food plays in our culture as opposed to the role it plays in less privileged cultures. Food is a major preoccupation wherever you go. In affluent cultures, however, people are not obsessed with food for its nutritional value so much as for the pleasure it gives. The story is quite different in cultures where hungry people need food for survival!

BULIMIA AND FOOD ADDICTION

In recent years, the eating disorders of anorexia and bulimia have become quite well-known and are often labeled as an addiction problem. Anorexia is characterized by a refusal to eat sufficient food while bulimia is episodic binge eating, usually while depressed, accompanied by a fear of not being able to stop eating. After the binge, the victim induces vomiting or takes laxatives to get rid of the food.

For those who are not familiar with these eating disorders, let me describe a typical case.

Samantha suffers from bulimia. At forty-two, she is married to a successful businessman. She is a homemaker with three daughters ranging in age from five to fifteen, but she is very dissatisfied with being "only" a mother and wife. She's done all the standard rounds of volunteer work—

hospital visitation, letter-stuffing at the church, committee work for the PTA, but she longs for a chance to do something "really meaningful." Her husband, however, insists that she needs to be at home.

So Samantha has become bulimic. She used to be anorexic; in her adolescent years she was preoccupied with thinness. Ever since she can remember, she feared becoming fat like her mother. She thought boys only liked very thin girls. So her life began to revolve around food—not its consumption, but its avoidance. She had problems with her menstrual periods, and she got sick often. The doctor kept telling her, "You're not eating enough. You're too thin for your age." Samantha would temporarily respond by eating regular meals, but would soon lapse into an anorexic mode again.

It was during one of these "normal" eating spells while in her teens that Samantha discovered how to induce vomiting. The feeling of fullness in her stomach was unpleasant, so she taught herself how to gag and throw up. From time to time she would purge herself with laxatives.

Samantha blamed her mother for a lot of her problems. She described her as domineering, intrusive, overbearing, and manipulative. As a child she had been forced into many activities (partly to fulfill her mother's unmet needs). Piano lessons, dance, and participation in a host of other programs left her exhausted much of the time. Over the years of her childhood, resentment toward her mother built up.

For several years in her twenties Samantha's eating problems subsided. Then, after giving birth to her third child, they started again. This time she became preoccupied with her weight. "I was so fat I had to do something," she explained to me later, showing me a photograph of herself at that time. She didn't look fat to me—but she thought she was.

Now Samantha's bulimia took over. She would binge whenever she was depressed or angry. Immediately after throwing up, she would become self-pitying, self-rejecting, withdrawn, and even more depressed or angry. It was a vicious cycle that would take much counseling to overcome.

Now my purpose in describing this case is to make the point that eating disorders like anorexia or bulimia are *not* the same as food addictions. In both anorexia and bulimia, food itself is not the primary problem. While there is a fascination with food, the preoccupation is with *avoiding it.* The person may feel out of control as far as food is concerned, but it is the underlying *emotional* disturbance that is the real problem, not the avoiding or eating of the food. Food avoidance is just a symptom of a much deeper problem. This is true for all addictions, but here the gap is too great to be considered the same.

One could argue that in bulimia the initial pleasure of eating still takes place and that this pleasure is itself addicting. True, this is possible. But in practice it never seems to work this way. Eating disorders are in a category all by themselves, not only in their symptoms, but also in their underlying dynamics. While it is very possible that some addictive elements may be present, they are not primarily disorders of addiction.

Therapy with bulimics can be extremely frustrating because they often want to focus only on the eating problem and resist facing the underlying emotional turmoil. It is these underlying problems that must be addressed in therapy. The eating problem will take care of itself when the underlying causes of self-hatred, shame, depression, and resentment have been resolved.

EATING STYLES THAT ARE ADDICTING

There are several "styles" of eating that can be addicting or contribute to an addiction problem:

1. *Overeating.* This seems the most obvious one to begin with. Despite our current cultural emphasis on physical health and slim appearance, many still overeat, and as a

result become obese. Those who overeat but never show it have a high metabolism and while their overeating may still be a potential addiction, they never suffer any serious consequences. Obesity, however, is a major problem that contributes significantly to other disorders like high blood pressure and diabetes, so it cannot be overlooked. National statistics on the prevalence of obesity estimate that between 20 and 30 percent of the population falls within this category.[1] Women have a greater tendency to be overweight than men.

While obesity can have several causes, including genetic predisposition and endocrine and biochemical disorders, mostly it is caused by too much energy going in and not enough coming out! It is all a matter of calorie arithmetic! At least, that is what we hear again and again much to the chagrin of people like myself who must constantly be on guard against overconsumption.

Underlying overeating, of course, is the complex drive we call "hunger." It is in this complex drive that the addictive features may lurk. We don't fully understand this phenomenon of craving. There is a physical hunger—a need for the nutrition that food provides—but many psychological factors cause hunger also. Family conflicts, sexual needs, personality problems, and tension can all contribute to a psychological need for food. We may seek nourishment or nurturing, pleasure or pacification. But the result is always the same. We overeat and if we do not have a high metabolism this can easily result in extra weight.

There is evidence that people who overeat often derive *less* pleasure from the normal activities that please nonobese people. In other words, food addicts don't get as much enjoyment from other activities as they get from eating. This makes sense, doesn't it? Nonaddicts are able to derive enjoyment from a wide variety of activities, not just food. This means that food is a very special source of pleasure and nurturing for those who have the potential to abuse it.

2. *Rapid Eating.* Fast eating may also be an addictive eating

"style." It is closely tied to personality and often applies to people with high adrenaline arousal such as Type-A people (always in a hurry, impatient, and easily angered) and workaholics. Both groups tend to gulp food and do not chew it well. As a result, they often have stomach problems.

3. *Snacking.* This is where I come in; I've been a snacker for years. It's a hard habit to break—an almost irresistible urge to have something in my mouth. I will often get up from dinner feeling quite satisfied and even satiated, only to begin the search for a snack an hour later.

Does this have the potential to become addicting? I believe so.

Most snack foods are high-calorie foods, so snacking can "feed" a significant weight problem and be a substitute for other forms of overeating. One way to reduce the impact of snacking is to substitute low-energy food. Nonfat yogurt, Weight Watchers snacks, and so forth have become a helpful replacement for me. I've even contemplated using lettuce as a snack at least as a temporary substitute for what has become a compulsive tendency—but somehow munching on that green stuff would never do it for me. I've chosen to go cold turkey instead to break the habit. This proves my point: We're looking for a fix when we snack, and this can lead to more serious problems in some cases.

4. *Situational Eating.* Certain situations may become the addictive core to eating. High-stress meetings, conflicts, deadlines, and any anxiety-producing demands may become linked with a need for food. The food helps to tranquilize the anxiety. This can easily lead to "situational" eating, in which you only overeat when you are under stress. The eating can take place before, during, or after the anxiety event, so it is not always easy to see how it is connected with the stress.

5. *Preloading.* Some people who anticipate that they may be without food will "preload"—or "stock up" either inside or outside the body. We may load up the pantry shelves or eat excessively ahead of time to carry us through. And for some

this preloading becomes addicting.

Preloaders are usually very insecure. They may have suffered from deprivation as children and thus formed an anticipatory anxiety associated with not being able to get food. When they go to a party, they are usually first in line at the food table. When they take a trip they stock up on food, "in case I get caught where there are no stores or restaurants." There is an actual fear of going hungry that demands careful planning. Of course, this is not limited to overeaters. Insecurity may cause a child to hoard food for emotional reasons, not so that it can be eaten. One twelve-year-old girl I worked with hoarded sandwiches in her clothes closet at the time her parents were divorcing. They were found uneaten, months later, moldy and rotten.

CATEGORIES OF FOOD THAT ARE ADDICTING

Not only do certain eating styles have the capability of being addicting, certain categories of food also have addicting properties. Often it is the *type* of food that creates the addicting *style*. This connection between the food type and eating style is important. Take the alcoholic, for example, who only wants to drink in a bar. The drinks he orders are pleasurable, of course, but the *style* of drinking also contributes to the overall pleasure. He can be "with the boys." He can enjoy familiar surroundings. These are all part of the addiction. Type and style cannot always be separated. This is also seen in high-sugar snacking at coffee breaks in work or school settings. The combination of collegial high spirits in a stressful environment can easily create an environment that is pleasurable and addicting in its own right.

The range of food that can be addicting is vast. I will limit myself to three that I frequently suspect as addictions: caffeine, sugar, and food additives.

Caffeine. Caffeine, of course, is not actually a food; it is a chemical found in such foods and beverages as coffee, tea, cocoa, and chocolate. It is also added to soft drinks and prescription and nonprescription drugs.

Caffeine ranks with alcohol and nicotine as one of the most widely used (and abused) mind-altering agents in our society. It is now well established that this substance has both acute and chronic effects on behavior, emotions, and body systems. And many people consume large amounts of it each day.

Have you ever kept a careful record of your caffeine intake? You will probably be surprised at how much you ingest. Here is a record kept by one of my clients. She reported, "I only had three cups of coffee. Not bad, huh?" She was startled when I pointed out how many other sources of caffeine she had consumed.

CAFFEINE DOSE

✔ 7 A.M.   1 cup of coffee
✔ 10 A.M.   1 cup of coffee
✔   1 chocolate donut or chocolate cake or chocolate candy bar
✔ 12 Noon Cola drink (containing caffeine) with lunch
✔ 3 P.M.   Headache medicine containing caffeine
✔   with a cup of strong tea
✔ 6 P.M.   1 cup of coffee with dinner
✔   Chocolate desert
✔ 9 P.M.   Snack of chocolate candy and
✔   a Cola drink

10 Total doses of caffeine

The total amount of caffeine one consumes, of course, differs according to the concentration of caffeine in the foods, drinks, and medications ingested. The amount in coffee, for instance, varies from country to country and from individual to individual depending on how strong you like it. You and I may both be drinking five cups of coffee a day, but I could be taking in three times as much caffeine because of the way I make it.

In recent months there have been some attempts in the news media to downplay the effects of caffeine. Whenever a research report states it is bad, I notice a counter-statement appears in a few months. It gives the appearance that researchers can't make up their minds. And it is true that news reports of this research (as with the value of oat bran and so forth in lowering cholesterol) have been confusing. First, researchers claimed that caffeine contributed to the risk for heart disease, then others refuted this. More recently it has been reported that it is the way the coffee is brewed that makes the difference: boiling is bad, dripping is good. Some reports recommended decaffeinated coffee; others labeled it poison.

Despite this confusion, I think the preponderance of evidence points to caffeine being a problem when consumed excessively. It is clearly a drug with recognizable effects, most of which are very familiar:

- *Caffeine stimulates the central nervous system.* Within half an hour you feel the effects of this stimulant—heart rate increased and blood pressure up.
- *Caffeine increases activity levels, reduces fatigue, and enhances alertness.* We use it to "wake us up."
- *Caffeine interferes with sleep.* You can't be stimulated and relaxed at the same time.
- *Caffeine increases the risk of panic attacks.* Anxiety sufferers can readily feel its effects.
- *Caffeine creates a state of high tension.* It puts you "on edge."

Cindy's reaction to coffee is typical of many anxiety sufferers I have seen over the years. She is thirty-nine years old, a mother of two teenage children, and active in church and community affairs.

She began her coffee habit in high school. All of her family members drink large amounts of it and she quickly learned its benefits. Many late nights of study could be managed with the help of black coffee. But she really didn't think she consumed a lot of coffee. "Usually two or three cups a day," she replied when I asked, but she never kept count; she drank it when she felt like it. When pressed, she conceded that in recent years her consumption has been more like four or five cups a day.

Several years ago Cindy began to suffer from "nervousness" and became quite anxiety-prone. Many things bothered her. She feared going out alone. She avoided people and social situations. She had headaches more often, and the doctor told her that her blood pressure was elevated.

Cindy's doctor referred her for a neurological evaluation— the usual brain scans and other tests. All was normal. Cindy was puzzled. "Could the problem be my coffee drinking?" she asked the doctor. Reluctantly he agreed this could be the problem, so Cindy decided to quit. This is when her real problems began. Her headaches got worse, not better, and she felt even more anxious. That is why she came to me for help.

I tried to break the news to Cindy gently. She was a caffeine "junkie"—there's no other way to put it. Like millions of Americans, she had become absolutely dependent on her drug. The problems she encountered when she tried to stop her coffee drinking were *withdrawal* symptoms.

What are the symptoms of caffeine withdrawal?

- *Headaches.* The body is used to the caffeine and revolts when it is lowered.
- *Fatigue.* The body is so accustomed to the stimulant of

caffeine that it has shut down its own natural stimulants. When the caffeine is removed, the body
experiences a dramatic letdown.

- *Depression.* The lowered adrenaline following reduction
  in caffeine starts a "postadrenaline" depression. One
  feels sad and unhappy.
- *Irritability.* The removal of caffeine leaves the addict
  easily angered and "on edge."
- *Increased stress*—at least initially. When you stop caffeine
  you first magnify the effects of stress on the cardio-
  vascular system. The heart skips beats or beats hard.
  Finally it settles down.

Together, these withdrawal symptoms can make life
pretty miserable.

The question you're probably asking right now is: "Am I
hooked on coffee (or tea, or colas)?" It's hard to give a
clear-cut answer. People differ in their tolerance for caffeine,
just as they do for alcohol or other drugs. You may drink six
or seven cups a day and not be an addict (although usually
more than five cups bespeaks an addiction). You may drink
two to three a day and be totally hooked! Your so-called cup
may actually be a mug that holds three cups!

The issue, of course, is not how much coffee or other
caffeine-loaded foods or beverages you ingest; the issue is
whether or not you are *dependent* on the caffeine. Here are
some important questions to ask yourself. The more times
you answer yes, the more likely you are to be addicted. (If
you are not a coffee drinker, substitute another caffeine-
loaded drink you drink often.)

- I cannot "get going" in the morning without having a
  cup or two of coffee.
- When I feel down, I usually drink a cup of coffee to perk
  me up.

- Whenever I go without coffee for a while, I get a headache.
- I couldn't easily stop drinking coffee.
- My heart races both when I drink coffee and when I haven't had any for a while.
- I drink more than five cups of coffee a day.

How can you break your caffeine addiction? First of all, you need to be convinced that caffeine is bad for you. Unless you believe this, you are not likely to change.

Once you are convinced you need to change, begin to reduce your caffeine intake *gradually*. You can go cold turkey if you want to, but severe withdrawal symptoms are best dealt with by gradual reduction of the caffeine. Cut out a half-cup or one cup a day, stay at that level for a few days, then reduce the amount further until you are down to an acceptable level or off the substance altogether. Then, if you associate the drink with a coffee break or other particular time and you find you miss the ritual, try substituting another beverage or food that does not contain caffeine. Decaffeinated coffee is a good substitute (although the jury is still out on whether it is clearly safe), as are mineral water, fruit juice, herbal tea, or just plain water! Stay on those substances, and you will be healthier, happier, and—most important—addiction free!

Sugar. The body has a love-hate relationship with sugar; if you believe everything you read in popular books and magazines. Sugar is generally considered "the killer on the breakfast table," and the underlying cause of everything from heart disease to hypoglycemia. And while some of the popular material may be exaggerated, I have no doubt that much food addiction revolves around our craving for the energy that simple sugars provide—whether directly through sugar-rich foods or refined sugar or indirectly through other foods.

Can we be addicted to starch (or complex carbohydrates)? Though all starch is easily changed into sugar in the intestine, this conversion is gradual and the sugar is released slowly. It therefore provides a sustained energy supply that is less addicting than the sudden "charge" refined sugar provides. Starches are, therefore, a better source of sugar than refined sugar is.

While we need sugar (and most of it can come from natural foods and not as refined sugar) in moderation as part of a balanced diet, too much refined sugar can overstimulate the production of insulin and digestive juices. It also interferes with the absorption of proteins, calcium, and many other minerals. The popular notion that we should cut back on our use of refined sugar and rely on other foods (fruit, whole-grain cereals, root vegetables, and so forth) to supply our sugar needs seems well founded. If we are hooked on it we may need to face up to possible withdrawal symptoms and some discomfort as we cut back. Taste buds may need to adapt themselves, over time, to less sweetness. As I have cut back, I notice that even small amounts of sugar can now taste quite sweet!

Food Additives. Because natural foods deteriorate quickly, preservatives are necessary. They have been a part of human experience from the dawn of history. Refrigerators and deep freezers are a very recent addition to human existence. Why, in my lifetime alone I can remember when electric refrigerators were a scarce luxury. My grandparents never had a refrigerator. They used a "cooler" that was kept outside. It was a large wooden box with walls of coke (a specially prepared coal) encased in wire mesh. Water constantly dripped from a reservoir above onto the top tray, and as it trickled through the coke it evaporated and cooled everything inside the box. As a young boy, I helped my grandfather build several of these coolers. It was much more fun than buying a refrigerator!

Food additives (such as nitrates and coloring substances), while they help to preserve and enhance food, clearly are chemicals. Many of these chemicals, especially those used to enhance color or taste, are suspects as cancer-causing agents. Hyperkinesis (excessive energy and movement, especially in children) and many other problems have been traced to certain food additives. This raises the possibility that certain additives may also have addicting properties.

Unfortunately we lack controlled studies and so much of our knowledge about the effect of these additives is anecdotal. No one has proven anything positively yet. This is not to say that we shouldn't avoid certain additives—it's just that we don't know conclusively which are really bad for us. We are at the mercy of whatever the Food and Drug Administration says! Some additives, like the sodium nitrate used to cure bacon, are important protectors from deadly food deterioration like botulism poisoning. It is a normal component of human saliva and comes naturally in many vegetables. This means that *little* amounts of this additive are probably healthy, even necessary. But how much is too much? I'm sorry to say that we really don't know.

Here again, you may have to decide for yourself. If you suspect an addiction to any additive or if you fear that some additive is bothering your system and creating unhealthy reactions, then take note of when you eat what and how you feel afterward. Clear patterns of reaction will begin to show up. Discuss these reactions with your physician.

OVERCOMING FOOD ADDICTIONS

The diagnosis of a food addiction is fairly easy to make. Too much dependence on food causes weight gain, and a careful review of how you use certain foods should give you a clear understanding of whether you are addicted or not.

Like adrenaline addiction, food addictions are especially

tricky to treat because we cannot easily go cold turkey. We can get along perfectly well without alcohol or cocaine—but we *need* food. Overcoming a food addiction, then, involves learning to live *with* food, not to live without it. (In the case of caffeine and additives, however, abstinence may well be possible and advisable.)

The first step in dealing with food addictions should be a physical examination; this will rule out endocrine or metabolic disorders or any other disease that could be causing changes in your eating patterns. Additionally, if you suffer from a severe case of food addiction or if your eating problem is out of control, you may need to see a psychiatrist or psychologist. Most weight-reduction programs tend to neglect the treatment of underlying emotional problems, which is why diet programs by themselves seldom bring about long-term permanent weight reduction when the cause lies in these underlying problems. Support groups like Weight Watchers, Overeaters Anonymous, and diet control centers provide accountability and mutual encouragement of the participants and are therefore very helpful for adjunct therapy. I strongly support these groups and encourage my patients to use them. But if you have a persistent problem with overeating and suspect some deeper emotional cause, consult a professional counselor or psychologist. You may be saving yourself a lot of unnecessary pain (and money) in the long run. Self-help seldom works here.

The use of appetite suppressants has gone out of vogue because these compounds are themselves addicting. (Appetite suppressants are usually amphetamine-based.) Such substances, if used, need to be carefully monitored by a licensed medical nutritionist or internist specializing in eating disorders. Never take an appetite suppressant without first consulting your physician!

Also, beware of fad diets. They can be dangerous, and because they usually offer "quick fixes" they are rarely effective in the long run. How can you tell if a diet fits this category? There are a few simple rules:

- It claims to be revolutionary.
- It reports testimonials rather than documented research.
- It claims 100 percent success.
- It claims persecution by the medical profession.

Any diet plan that has these four characteristics should be treated with suspicion. Fad diets have come and gone for years; I marvel at the public's gullibility in believing almost anything about dieting. On the whole, liquid diets, low-protein diets, high-protein diets, grapefruit diets, the hard-boiled-egg diets, and all "amazing" diets only amass profits for their promoters. At best, they charge money for weight you would lose anyway. At worst, they can be dangerous.

How should you lose weight, then? Assuming you are also dealing with the underlying emotional problems that caused your problem in the first place, there are only a few basic principles that should be followed:

- *Remember, losing weight is a matter of arithmetic.* A diet that provides *fewer* calories than you expend will cause weight loss. You must either eat less or exercise more; there is no other way to control weight.
- *Regular eating habits should include a balance of fruits, vegetables, whole grains, and other basic foods.*
- *Portion size—not the type of food—is the key.*
- *Exercise not only reduces weight; it provides many other benefits as well—including reduced stress.*

One important word of caution I must sound concerns a possible addiction to "noneating." I'm not sure that this has ever been documented in the research literature, but I am convinced that one can become addicted to states of deprivation. Starving oneself can produce an "altered state"; we know this to be the case in hypoglycemia (low blood sugar). Since stringent diets can create these altered states, they have the potential to become a form of addiction. Elements of self-punishment and masochism may play a part in perpetual dieting.

Beyond the *mechanics* of dieting, there are other important issues to be addressed in food addictions as well:

1. *Identify the "triggers" that can set off addictive behavior.* These include a sense of failure, rejection, and criticism. Develop strategies for dealing with these directly, not through food.

2. *Beware of the trap of competitiveness.* All addicts are especially vulnerable to competitive standards and comparisons. We compare ourselves with others all the time in our culture and always come up feeling inadequate. There will always be someone you can identify as better or worse!

3. *Learn how to adjust to change and adapt flexibly to new pressures.* Rigidity tends to foster resistance to change, and this creates more stress and tension. If we don't "bend" with the wind of change, we will surely ʰreak—or an addiction will break us.

4. *Listen to your "inner" feelings and the messages they convey to you.* Don't deny them or shut them out; they are your friends. You will be altogether healthier if you know how to "free" your feelings.

5. *Accept your imperfections.* After all, you are only human. Have the courage to face and honor your faults and deficiencies. We *all* suffer from blemishes of one sort or another. The more accepting we are of this, the less likely we are to use food or any other substance to pacify our dissatisfaction with ourselves.

Problems with food are not a modern phenomenon. Scripture warns us not to misuse our appetites (Phil 3:19) and states clearly that food does not bring us nearer to God (1 Cor 8:8). Can any advice be healthier than Paul's?

Whether therefore ye eat, or drink, or whatsoever ye do, do all to the glory of God. 1 Cor 10:31

PART III

Healing for
Hidden Addictions

TWELVE

Overcoming Your Hidden Addiction

I N A WAY, OVERCOMING AN ADDICTION is like learning a sport. Each sport—golf, tennis, or bowling—requires mastering specific skills. You must learn how to stand, how to address the ball, how to swing your arms. But there are also *general* skills that are universally applicable. You must maintain physical fitness and develop mental alertness, quick reflexes, and a playful spirit.

The same is true of healing hidden addictions; there are general skills to be learned. This chapter will deal with these in the realm of the physical and psychological, while the next and last chapters will focus on spiritual issues. This separation, however, is only for clarity in presentation. I trust you understand that we really cannot separate spiritual issues from physical or psychological aspects of our being. We function as a whole—and God deals with us in our totality.

THE SEARCH FOR SELF IN OUR HIDDEN ADDICTIONS

What really lies at the root of our need to be perfect, happy, fulfilled, or "actualized"? What is the real reason we become workaholics, obsessional gamblers, or fitness junkies? I think it's because we are all on a search for ourselves—for our true selves. To be human is to be self-aware, to be conscious of one's self. This awareness means we are capable of setting up an "ideal" image for ourselves and of constantly evaluating how closely we measure up to it. This can be deeply satisfying, but it can also be the source of much self-rejection. It causes us either to escape from this self-realization or to overcompensate for our shortfall. Either road is potholed with addictive hazards.

The quest for an "ideal" self is an obsession held by modern people. The image we seek to measure up to is a "perfect" image. Often this image is shaped by our sub-culture. Reflect for a moment on the dimensions of this search:

1. *The "perfect" body.* We long to have perfect bodies—not just for health and longevity, but to live up to the ideals of our culture. For Americans in the latter part of the twentieth century this usually means sleek, unblemished, slender, and athletic-looking—the image portrayed in ads and the media.

2. *The "perfect" psyche.* Our ideal image also includes having a perfect personality and complete mastery of all unpleasant emotions. We desire to have a dynamic charisma so that people will like us and ultimately meet all our needs. To achieve this, many people go to therapy or take courses to improve their self-esteem and build their confidence.

3. *The "perfect" spirit.* In recent years the quest for spiritual perfection has received new emphasis through the New Age movement. Many people have become obsessed with finding perfect peace, perfect ecstasy, "being at one with the universe"—and many New Age leaders promise to show them how. And of course, there's a Christian version of this search. Believers look toward the ideal image of a "perfect Christian" who prays constantly, studies the Bible intensely, supports the church, and witnesses effectively.

Understanding and overcoming these quests for a perfect

body, psyche, or spirit is essential if we want to be freed from addiction or to avoid developing an addiction.

Let me focus for a moment on our addiction to pursuing a perfect body and its most common form: physical fitness. It illustrates for me where and how we need to straighten out our thinking about wanting things to be "perfect." A serious commitment to fitness *can* be a very positive thing. When our bodies are in good running order, our minds are usually sharper and our spirits more at peace. But a preoccupation with fitness (which can be an addiction root) can be a way of denying our mortality, of refusing to face up to the inevitable aging process and our final departure from this life. This denial of aging and death is inherently unhealthy because it feeds our refusal to face reality.

Many of us, however, continue to deny the reality of life's finiteness. This is the whole point of Ernest Becker's marvelous book, *The Denial of Death!*[1] The fear of death, or "terror" as he calls it, is ever-present with us but pushed out of awareness or repressed. In normal times we move about without actually believing in our own death. Irrationally, we think we can somehow master death by having a good time, by experiencing all the thrills life can give, or by dulling our senses with drugs or tranquilizing activity. But in running away from our awareness of our mortality, we also fail to be our true selves.

What is the "ideal" of mental and spiritual health, then? Ernest Becker sums it up like this: "A lived, compelling illusion [he really means vision] that does not lie about life, death, and reality; one honest enough to follow its own commandments."[2]

Becker was not a Christian, but his answer gets to the heart of healthy living. If we want to be physically, psychologically, and spiritually healthy, *we must not lie* about life, death, and reality. And all addictions have this in common: *They lie about reality.* They deceive us into thinking that through the addictive activity we can somehow make things better or get what we want as we escape from reality.

On the matter of our lying about reality in our search for a perfect psyche, Ernest Becker also has some sobering things to say about psychotherapy. Since so many addictions lead us to psychotherapy as a way of healing (and I am a strong advocate of Christian psychotherapy, since I truly believe this is my calling from God), we need to be reminded periodically of its limitations.

Becker agrees that psychotherapy can give great gifts to tortured and overwhelmed people. It can give insight to those who thirst for self-knowledge. (I would add that it can also remove obstacles to letting God's Spirit work within you, smash the idols that keep self-esteem low, and lift the load of neurotic guilt.) But as Becker points out, "there are many things [psychotherapy] cannot do."[3] Often psychotherapy promises the moon. It seems to offer a more constant joy and "perfect" freedom. But often, instead, it simply lays reality bare—and reality is not always happy: "Not everyone is as honest as Freud was when he said that he cured the miseries of the neurotic only to open him up to the normal misery of life."[4]

What an insight! Why is it so often overlooked or ignored by psychotherapists—Christian or otherwise? We ought to put up a small sign on all therapists' doors:

Danger: real probability of the awakening of terror and dread, from which there is no going back.[5]

We should all be very aware of how much terror can be created when you take away normal defenses and probe deep into the psyche. Paradise through self-knowledge is a myth, as is the hope that some substance or activity will change your life. The only road to peace and freedom from all addictions is the road that goes by a cross on which God's Holy Lamb was slain. Christ frees us from our fear of death (and thus our fear of living also) because, in him, "death is swallowed up in victory" (1 Cor 15:54).

With the fear of death and avoidance of life's realities put away, you can begin to become a "true self." You can begin to heal your fragmentation, remove the things that are blocking you from a full life, and discover real joy, the joy of finding more of yourself and throwing off your self-defeating tendencies. Physical fitness, or any other pastime or pursuit, then becomes a way of fulfilling God's plan for your life, and mental health merely a means for knowing God more fully. Addictions find no foothold in such a life.

HOW DO YOU SEE YOURSELF?

Since a search for self lies behind many addictions, it is important for each of us to ask, "How do I see myself?" Our "self-image"—how we perceive our intellect, physique, competence, attractiveness, and acceptance by others—is the foundation for self-esteem. A poor self-image, therefore, is a major source of anxiety and depression. We worry about what people think about us, and this worry can make us depressed. We are not "free" until we break the hold that a fear of what people think has over us.

As you reflect on your self-image, you are bound to identify aspects of yourself that you don't like. In our culture, with its excessive competitiveness and emphasis on performance, a person can't help growing up without feeling deficient in some areas. Perhaps the external representation of your inner self, your physique or appearance, is your major disappointment. Perhaps you feel you are not intelligent enough. You name it—there will be scores of people who feel inadequate in that area. This is a fact of life in our culture. We all come into adulthood feeling that we fall short of the ideal, and to some extent we do. This is why the Christian gospel is such a powerful antidote for the poison of low self-esteem. Because God accepts us for what we are, we can begin to accept our basic imperfections. The gospel's call to "be perfect" is not a call to becoming a perfect self but a call to take off the filthy rags of self-righteousness and put on the righteousness of Christ. We trade cloaks! Our perfection is "in Christ," not in being an outstanding athlete or a beautiful person.

This then leads me to ask the all important question: *What is wrong with being imperfect?* Why do we fear it so? Why does failure devastate us? Why do we have an exaggerated need to have a perfect face, body, intellect, personality, or spirit? Is it because a person cannot be happy without being perfect? I don't think so. I know many happy people, and not one of them is perfect, although it is easy to fall into the trap of thinking they are!

Is it because being perfect would make us better than others? I suspect this gets nearer to the truth. Not only is this part of what it means to be sinful by nature, but we are taught from childhood that we must be in competition with each other; we must make it to the top of the class or to be the most outstanding athlete. If these motivating forces were limited to helping us realize our best potential, they would be healthy, but unfortunately they go further. We feel inadequate because we compare ourselves with others. We feel like failures when someone else comes out better than us, whether or not we have reached our fullest potential. And this sets us up for trouble, because the harder we try, we can always find someone who is better than we are!

I consider it to be an essential component of mental and spiritual health that we develop the "courage to be imperfect." By this I don't mean that we should be content to be a nothing, or that we should resign ourselves to mediocrity. Not at all. I believe God calls us to become the best we can be. This is clearly the teaching of the parable of the talents (Mt 25:14-30). If we are "behind" because we haven't yet reached our fullest potential, then God expects us to go the extra mile and try to get there.

But we need to realize that even when we have tried our best and reached our ultimate potential, we will *still be imperfect*. Others will be better than us. Can we accept this? Others will be stronger, prettier, smarter, more handsome, taller, more successful, better preachers and therapists than we are. Can we give them the right to be this way? And these people will be imperfect, too. Our healthiness is then determined by whether or not we can accept that we and everyone else is imperfect. This is the truth of the human condition. If we can, we can depend on God's help and can be happy and blessed in this acceptance. If we can't, we will remain discontented and, who knows, perhaps more prone to addictions.

Later in this chapter I will discuss the twelve steps to recovery that are widely used in many addiction recovery programs (Alcoholics Anonymous, Overeaters Anonymous, and so on). The twelve-step programs all emphasize awareness and acceptance of our imperfections, powerlessness, and basic sinfulness. I think this emphasis is one reason these programs are so successful.

But accepting the fact that you are imperfect doesn't mean that you should not grow or change. Generally speaking, our imperfections fall into two categories: imperfections we can fix and imperfections that are unfixable. If my wife tells me that I have become quick-tempered because I am under a lot of pressure at work, I don't respond by saying, "Sorry, honey, but that's the way I am! I accept myself like this so you must also." No! Love compels me to try to take control and change my quick temper, no matter how tolerant of my weakness she may be. However, if I feel that being short in height (as I am) is clearly not an asset and that I should not accept myself until I do something about this, I am creating an impossible bind. There is nothing to change here. If I feel that this is an imperfection (and I question whether it is), then I need to just accept it, change my attitude toward it, and get on with my life. This is true whether my imperfection involves my intelligence, my abilities, or the size of my feet. Of course, these are muddy waters here. Who can say whether something can or cannot be changed sometimes? You must be open to what those closest to you have to say about this.

The apostle Paul understood well this need to keep striving for change while having the courage to accept what cannot be changed:

> I don't mean to say I am perfect. I haven't learned all I should even yet, but I keep working toward that day when I will finally be all that Christ saved me for and wants me to be. Phil 3:12 LB

GENERAL TECHNIQUES FOR OVERCOMING HIDDEN ADDICTIONS

Four general techniques are absolutely necessary to learn if you want to overcome your hidden addiction. (I think these skills are also helpful in substance addictions.) They are: relaxation, stress control, cognitive restructuring, and increasing tolerance for frustration.

Relaxation. In recent years we have rediscovered the value of relaxation. Research has clearly shown that deep muscle relaxation is profoundly effective in lowering adrenaline and cortisol, the two main stress hormones. Relaxation also helps build up the brain's supply of natural tranquilizers. In fact, I can't think of anything that is not helped by the ability to relax, including our temperament.

Unfortunately, relaxing is hard for many of us. The more stressed and driven we become, the more difficult it is to take the time for relaxation, and the more uncomfortable we feel when we try to relax. That is why a deliberate relaxation routine can be helpful.

Now, the kind of relaxation that is beneficial does not take a lot of time. Twenty or thirty minutes of effective relaxation a day is all it takes to begin the miraculous transformation of your body. While I provide a more complete description of a relaxation technique elsewhere,[6] let me briefly describe the process:

1. *Sit or lie in a comfortable position.* Make sure you cannot be disturbed (hang a sign on the door if necessary). Any time of the day is acceptable.

2. *Set a timer* for twenty to thirty minutes and give yourself to the relaxation exercise. Try to forget about appointments or tasks waiting to be done. (If you find it hard to do this, keep a pad and pencil next to you. When a troublesome thought intrudes, write it down, then return to your relaxation. You can take care of it after you are through relaxing.)

3. *Don't fall asleep.* If you do, your problem is probably not a need for relaxation but a lack of adequate sleep. You may want to read chapter 11 of my book on stress about this.[7]

4. *Progressively tense and relax your muscles.* Starting at your feet and working up the body, first tighten each muscle group for five seconds, then relax it and *leave the muscles relaxed.*

5. *Lie or sit still once you've worked your way through all the muscle groups.* Slowly your muscle tension will subside. This inactivity may feel very uncomfortable at first, but after four or five sessions it will begin to feel wonderful. Chances are, the more uncomfortable you feel when you try to relax, the more you need the relaxation!

6. *Avoid troublesome thoughts.* If you like, you can mentally quote Scripture or recite hymns, or you can just think of something relaxing and pleasant. Do not speak or sing out loud, however; these activities use muscles.

7. *At the end of your allotted time, go about your business* but continue to think "relaxation" all through your day.

Stress Control. I call the particular form of stress control I espouse-"adrenaline management" because it centers on what I believe is the essence of stress—adrenaline over-arousal.[8] Most of us simply do *not* need as much adrenaline as we think we do. Adrenaline is for emergencies, not for everyday living, but we easily come to think we need its "rush" to cope with our ordinary challenges—meeting deadlines, handling conflict, facing traffic, reprimanding children, and so on. This is why so much about stress can be addicting to us.

Stress control, then, is essentially a matter of lowering adrenaline. Several techniques are useful:

1. *Controlling "self-talk."* We can calm ourselves through reassuring self-statements such as, "I don't need to be angry right now. I'll deal with this in due course."

2. *Planning ahead for periods of high demand.* If you have a major conflict coming up, cut back on your other activities so that you don't deplete your adrenaline reserves. You'll need all you've got for the major conflict.

3. *Building in recovery time.* My own life changed when I finally realized that I need to plan for "recovery time" after periods of high adrenaline arousal. In other words, if I know that I will be "under the gun" with heavy demands, I try to block out a time of rest and reduced demands afterward. This requires assertiveness; one needs to learn to say no and to insist that every demanding task needs its subsequent "sabbatical" or rest.

4. *Avoid the adrenaline emotions*—anger, resentment, frustration, and irritation. These emotions recruit adrenaline for "fight or flight" and thus increase stress levels. Try to develop a calm and quiet spirit. In particular, avoid getting angry easily. Anger is a very primitive emotion. Its purpose is to tell you that you feel violated and out of control. It also raises blood pressure and causes stress damage to the heart.

5. *Develop alternative ways of dealing with pressure.* We cannot always avoid stress, but we can diffuse it by enhancing certain "natural tranquilizers." Here are some suggestions:

- *Use laughter to diffuse stress.* Try to develop a humorous outlook, to take things less seriously. Humor puts things in perspective and relieves the tension of a difficult situation. It also keeps us humble—and lovable.

- *Use music to "soothe [your] savage beast."* Relaxation music is better for you than TV programs with car chases and excitement. The music should be slow, quiet, nonvocal. If it bores you, it's probably good as a tranquilizer!
- *Talk out your frustrations.* We were created with the capacity to share our feelings and our burdens. Talk to someone who listens and offer to be a good listener in return. Writing down your feelings can also help clarify them and reduce tension. *And* remember, God wants to hear what we feel as much as he wants to hear what we want.

Cognitive Restructuring. This general technique is quite simple to apply. Essentially, it is a way of *changing how we view situations.* For instance, let's suppose I come home late in the evening without having told my wife I would be late. As I walk in, my wife is waiting by the door, furious; she has had dinner on the table for an hour and a half. She feels uncared for: "If you really loved me, you would tell me you are coming home late." She feels devalued: "Is this how much I mean to you?" I think I can leave you to fill in the rest of the heated exchange.

Now, I could react in anger. I could loudly protest, "Don't you remember last month when I told you I would be late tonight? It is written on the calendar! See for yourself!" I could feel very self-righteous and point to the star next to today's date on the Savings and Loan calendar just above the telephone. I could feel aggrieved. "Why should I have to remember to tell you everything when it is written down?"

Alternatively I could "restructure my thinking." I could remind myself that my wife is angry because she feels that my lack of adequate communication represented a lack of caring. It could also be because she is afraid. To her, my absence could mean I've had an accident or even been mugged—anything. Her anger is a reflection of her love and care for me. Don't I want her to care for me? Why should I retaliate with anger when all she is doing is showing me how much I mean to her?

So, by restructuring my thinking and redefining what is going on, I avoid further conflict and help to reduce my stress. I also help my wife to love me more.

To be able to do this is essential to mental health. Things are not always as they seem, and we need to constantly be evaluating our thoughts and to avoid creating problems in our head.

Increasing Frustration Tolerance. A low tolerance for frustration is characteristic of all addicts, process or substance. Any delay in satisfying a need or obstacle that slows them down sets up an anxiety or anger reaction. When they want something, they want it *now. They want immediate rewards, not delayed ones.*

This low tolerance for frustration or blocked goals creates a high level of aggression. A person, therefore, who wants a need to be gratified *immediately* but encounters a barrier of some kind becomes frustrated, aggressive, or angry. The barrier may be physical, psychological, or symbolic, and the aggression is designed to get around the barrier. The victim, therefore, becomes *less* logical, *more* irrational, and *more* emotional than would usually be the case.

To avoid this frustration, people with low tolerance turn to addictions, either to help them avoid the frustration (for instance, blotting out awareness of the blocked goal) or to help them achieve their goal. Some workaholics, for example, are persons with a low tolerance for frustration who must work unceasingly to get what they want as quickly as possible. They can't wait like the rest of us for the good things of life. They are too impatient.

What can you do about a low tolerance for frustration? Several things:

1. *Accept that your impulsiveness is not a healthy way of going about things.* Reason with yourself until you believe that you don't have to get things now or have your way every time.

2. *Discipline your attitude to frustration by* **choosing** *situations that are frustrating.* If, like me, you tend to be impatient with delays at the supermarket, then intentionally choose the longest line as a way of teaching yourself to accept delays.

I have learned that this can be a great spiritual experience. Because you have *chosen* the action, you don't feel angry. The discipline brings its own reward—a deep satisfaction from knowing you are in control of yourself.

3. *Pray about your low frustration tolerance.* God can free you from this weakness. If you let him, he can give you patience and long-suffering to make up what you lack. This is the message of the apostle James:

Dear brothers [and sisters], is your life full of difficulties and temptations? Then be happy, for when the way is rough, your patience has a chance to grow. So let it grow, and don't try to squirm out of your problems. For when your patience is finally in full bloom, then you will be ready for anything, strong in character, full and complete.

Js 1:2-3 LB

Many personality problems can be rectified by more intentional spiritual discipline. But this does not mean that God will always remove the problem. More often, he offers the power to help us discipline ourselves, choose the right action, and follow through on the right behavior. His power is given to us to help us *overcome* the problem and learn from the experience, not to provide a shortcut to perfection. Rather than doing the work for us, he provides us with the tools; it is up to us to use them. This is the meaning of

Philippians 2:13: "For God is at work within you, helping you want to obey him, and then helping you do what he wants" (LB).

TWELVE-STEP PROGRAMS

No discussion of how to overcome an addiction would be complete without some comments about *twelve-step programs*. In fact, it is surprising to me how little is known by average Christians about these programs.

What are the "twelve steps"? They are a model "spiritual program of recovery" developed by the founders of Alcoholics Anonymous (AA). These steps have helped literally millions of people conquer their addiction problems—both substance and nonsubstance. In fact, no other program of recovery has been as effective in helping people overcome addictions as those based on the twelve-step principles. They have also been applied to compulsive behavior patterns, codependency problems, and even marital conflicts. (A list of twelve-step organizations is found in the appendix.)

There is some ambivalence in more conservative Christian circles about these programs. These critics object that these programs are not Christ-centered enough. And to a certain extent this is true. Most twelve-step organizations, trying to reach as many people as possible, avoid specifically Christian doctrine and terminology, using terms, for instance, like "higher power" and "God as you understand him" to refer to the deity.

But the fact that the twelve steps can be used in secular settings should not discourage their use in a Christian setting. I happen to believe that when the twelve steps are followed in genuine dependence on the living God, they become an even more powerful set of tools that God can use for our healing. But even when used in their secular setting, the twelve steps have brought many into an experience of

God's grace. For those who have accomplished their recovery without really coming to know the true God I feel some regret, but I certainly would not begrudge them their recovery.

The origin of the twelve steps was clearly Christian. Bill Wilson, a man who struggled with alcohol during the 1920s and 1930s, came under the influence of the Oxford Group, an aggressively evangelical movement in England whose members had a knack for reaching the down-and-out with the gospel. He committed his life to the Christ they told him about, and the miracle happened: He got sober, and he stayed sober. So did some of his alcoholic friends. Soon there was a group of recovering alcoholics supporting each other. The twelve steps were formulated and honed out of the experience of that group.

A summary of these steps is as follows (AA does not like the full text of the steps to be published; I have given just enough of them to give an idea of the process):

1. We admit we are powerless over certain areas of our lives.
2. We believe that a power greater than ourselves can restore our wholeness.
3. We decide to turn our lives over to God.
4. We make a searching moral inventory.
5. We admit our shortcomings to God, to ourselves, and to others.
6. We prepare to let God remove all our defects.
7. We ask God to transform our weaknesses.
8. We list all people we have harmed and become willing to make amends.
9. We make amends wherever possible.
10. We continue to take a regular personal inventory.
11. We seek through prayer to improve our relationship with God.
12. We call others to practice these principles as well.

A publication called *Pastoral Renewal*[9] provides an excellent review of twelve-step programs. Not only does this journal describe how they work; it also examines both the extent to which they are Christian and their place in pastoral care. In addition, the Minnesota-based Institute for Christian Living (ICL) has adapted the twelve steps back to a more basic Christian foundation.[10] ICL's version of the twelve steps centers more directly on the need for salvation, dependence on the Holy Spirit, and the development of a spirituality that is more patently Christian:

1. We admit our need for God's gift of salvation—that we are powerless over certain areas of our lives and that our lives are at times sinful and unmanageable.
2. We come to believe through the Holy Spirit that a power who came in the person of Jesus Christ and who is greater than ourselves can transform our weaknesses into strengths.
3. We make a decision to turn our will and our lives over to the care of Jesus Christ as we understand him—hoping to understand him more fully.
4. We make a searching and fearless moral inventory of ourselves—both our strengths and weaknesses.
5. We admit to Christ, to ourselves, and to another human being the exact nature of our sins.
6. We become entirely ready to have Christ heal all of these defects of character that prevent us from having a more spiritual lifestyle.
7. We humbly ask Christ to transform all of our short-comings.
8. We make a list of all persons we have harmed and become willing to make amends to them all.
9. We make direct amends to such persons whenever possible except when to do so would injure them or others.
10. We continue to take personal inventory and when we

are wrong, promptly admit it and, when we are right, thank God for the guidance.

11. We seek through prayer and meditation to improve our conscious contact with Jesus Christ as we understand him, praying for knowledge of God's will for us and the power to carry that out.

12. Having experienced a new sense of spirituality as a result of these steps and realizing that this is a gift of God's grace, we are willing to share the message of Christ's love and forgiveness with others and to practice these principles for spiritual living in all our affairs.

There are several ways you can use these steps. One way is to follow through on them by yourself, taking each one at a time. The second—and more effective—way is to band together with a group of other believing Christians and seek out the assistance of someone who has "worked the steps" in another recovery program. You cannot learn the process from a book—you need someone to guide you through the steps.

Group Support. The appeal and widespread success of "working the steps" is due to its ability to help people get at the core of their problems. A large factor in that success, however, is group support; it provides a system in which members are held accountable to one another and to God.

Recovered alcoholics will tell you that they needed this support almost every day at first to keep them on the road to recovery. *Stopping* an addiction is relatively easy. Anyone can stop smoking, gambling, working excessively, or overeating. The challenge is to *stay stopped.* This is where the group support and twelve steps come in. They help people to accept the true nature of their problem, get at the root dysfunction, admit their human powerlessness to change, and then use God's resources to change anyway. All of this is done in the context of people helping people.

Mutually supportive groups are effective for a number of reasons:

- Meeting other people with similar problems helps you feel less alone.
- Knowing what other group members are experiencing builds a sense of confidence.
- In helping others, you really help yourself more.
- Being in a group helps you break denial.
- Being in a group helps you quit blaming others or circumstances for your problems.
- Other group members serve as significant social reinforcers for positive change.

I would strongly advocate, then, whether you are endeavoring to help yourself through sheer willpower, through some modification of a twelve-step program, or through psychotherapy, that you involve yourself in a support group of some kind. Many Christians fear that sharing one's struggles with another is a sign of failure. But "burden sharing" is a thoroughly biblical idea. In fact, Paul directly admonished the Galatians to "share each other's troubles and problems, and so obey our Lord's command. If anyone thinks he is too great to stoop to this, he is fooling himself. He is really a nobody" (Gal 6:2-3 LB).

At the root of all twelve-step programs is the concept of *accountability* to God through another human. All programs of spiritual counseling work on this principle also. It's not that the other person gives us strength or usurps God's place. It is simply a fact that we grow fastest when we hold ourselves responsible to one another.

Taking It Slowly. AA members and others following the traditional twelve-step programs make a point of not rushing the process of recovery. Abstinence is required up front, but reaching the fourth step (making a fearless and searching moral inventory) often takes four or five years. The reason for this is obvious: Such a painful step cannot be taken without preparation. Getting ready for total self-honesty takes time. (How *much* time it takes depends on the depth of one's denial and the degree of self-honesty that has naturally developed.)

Before you can face yourself starkly and be stripped of all pretenses, you need to take time to work the first three steps: admitting your powerlessness (and for the Christian this means also sinfulness), believing that God through his Holy Spirit can empower you and transform your weakness into strength, and deciding to turn yourself over to him. You may need to do these things over and over before you are ready to go forward.

Because the early steps can be so difficult and take so much time, twelve-step organizations try to pair beginners up with a "sponsor" who is further along in the process of recovery. This is a good practice to adopt whether or not you are involved in one of these programs. Someone who is a little further down the road to recovery can help you avoid pitfalls and encourage you when you are down. He or she can also be a spiritual adviser.

I strongly recommend that you also slow down and take the time to bring yourself to a full understanding of these "entry" steps. This may be painful and lengthy, but God is there to help you do this. A friend's listening ear or a counselor's skill can speed up the process, but it cannot be short-circuited.

Steps four through ten are basically a program of repentance and restitution. What can be more biblical? I urge you, therefore, to reflect on each of these steps *when you are ready,* and then with good counsel implement them *carefully.*

I add this caution because "gaining a clear conscience" can sometimes be destructive—a matter of dumping one's guilt on someone else, who is then left to carry the pain of your actions. It's not that one shouldn't confess to others. It is a matter of *how* and *when* you do it.

Say, for example, you have a sensitive and fragile spouse. She feels very insecure and is easily upset. You decide you want to clear your conscience about some extramarital fling. Your wife knows nothing about this, and you suspect she will be very upset by the confession. *Don't* just go and dump it on her. One husband I know did this to his sick wife with devastating consequences; she plunged into a deep depression. When I challenged him about his callous confession, his response was: "Well, that's her problem. I did what I had to do! I got it off my chest."

That kind of confession is hardly the action of love if it does not bring ultimate healing or if it is an act of revenge. I would have advised that man to seek the counsel of an understanding friend or pastor first, to think through the consequences and weigh the options. Perhaps some other action could have been taken *before* the confession took place, such as an effort at strengthening the relationship and the spouse's self-esteem with acts of love. Or perhaps the confession could have been delayed until the spouse was recovered from her illness.

Before carrying out the steps of confessing and making restitution, I suggest that you ask yourself several questions: What purpose would the confession serve? Is it something I should confess only to God? What is my motive for confessing? Do I merely want to hurt the person I'm confessing to? These questions need to be carefully evaluated and God's wisdom sought. Only he can give us the absolutely right direction in such ticklish dilemmas.

An Ongoing Process. "Working the steps" was never intended to be a one-time process—just as confession, repentance, and restitution is never a once-and-for-all activity. The Christian life is like so many board games: you go round and round, passing through the starting point again and again. (The difference, of course, is that each time around brings greater depth and understanding, and the whole process leads somewhere.)

Steps ten through twelve emphasize this "continuation" process, which is carried out through prayer and meditation and also involves sharing this walk with others.

The process is not easy; in fact, it involves a great deal of *pain* at every step. Confessions can be demoralizing. Repentance is inherently humiliating. Making amends can be costly, not just in terms of time or money, but in emotional sweat and tears.

This *pain* is part of the program, I am sorry to say; there can be no sustained spiritual or psychological growth without it. Remember, many addictions are an attempt to avoid deep, hurting pain, so overcoming those addictions means facing that pain. Life can be terrifying at times, and it can become even more frightening near the end. But nothing of real value is gained without effort and pain.

The fact that pain is inevitable, however, doesn't mean it is insurmountable. I recently counseled with a well-established businessman whose business was about to go under. All his life he feared this would happen, and now his failure was staring him in the face. His first reaction had been to consider suicide—painful, to be sure, but quickly over. Then, he tells me, a great sense of peace came over him. It happened when he realized he was powerless to control his destiny, that only God could have any influence over the catastrophe in his life. The moment that truth dawned on him, he surrendered everything to God, and a great peace came over him; he felt no more anxiety or panic. He still had a lot to do, but he could now proceed to do it with the assurance that he was not alone.

As this man shared this story with me, my mind raced immediately to the words of King David in Psalm 4:

Many say that God will never help us. Prove them wrong, O Lord, by letting the light of your face shine down upon us.... I will lie down in peace and sleep, for though I am alone, O Lord, you will keep me safe. Ps 4:6, 8 LB

Unless your program of recovery can bring this peace, it is not giving you God's best. Many have proven God's critics to be wrong. We *do* lie down in peace and sleep when we let his face shine upon us.

THE VALUE OF PROFESSIONAL HELP

I cannot close this chapter without emphasizing the value of professional help, especially if your addiction is likely to be harmful to others.

I once encountered a pastor who had advised a parishioner with a sexual addiction that involved small children not to seek professional help. He told the man "to go home and pray about it." He assured the parishioner it would "all come right" if he confessed his sin and repented. Many months later this parishioner was discovered sexually abusing his five-year-old granddaughter! The damage to that child is almost irreparable. She will carry that scar the rest of her life, and no amount of punishment can compensate for the damage that man caused.

I hold that pastor partly accountable for the violation. He acted negligently, and his only excuse was ignorance. Unfortunately, this is not an isolated case; I hear horror stories all the time about well-meaning people who give the wrong advice.

What does good professional help offer? Certainly not a perfect cure for every problem. But it does provide expert help in:

- understanding the nature of addiction,
- getting to the underlying reasons for the addiction,

- forcing the addict to be accountable to an "authority" person,
- forcing honest self-reflection and self-examination,
- helping evaluate progress in recovery.

If the professional is a Christian, the relationship also provides spiritual support through prayer and fellowship in God's Spirit. Generally, I strongly recommend that you first seek a Christian professional's help. However, do not do this at the expense of competence. The appendix provides resources to help you locate this kind of professional help in your area.

THIRTEEN

A Theology for Self-Control

"YOU WILL NOT OVERCOME an addiction by willpower alone." These are the words of a patient of mine, a recovering alcoholic. "The harder you try, the easier you fall back. Forcing yourself to stop only drives you further into the addiction."

These are true words, spoken out of the depth of personal agony. (This man had a strong addiction to unusual sexual practices in addition to his alcoholism.) After twenty years of struggle, he now feels he is finally "in control." But this control has come more from his reliance upon and openness to the work of the Holy Spirit in his life than on his force of will.

The issue of choice and control can be a confusing one for addicts. Even though willpower alone won't overcome an addiction, all addictions are still "diseases of choice." Once an addiction is well-entrenched, it may well feel uncontrollable; this lack of control is one of the characteristics of an addiction. But recovery can only begin when a *decision* is made to begin the recovery process. This decision always remains in the hands of the addict.

Issues of free will and responsibility must therefore play a major role in understanding how to bring our hidden addictions under control. At some point in time the addict *chose* to do the addicting thing. A time must come again when the addict chooses to begin the healing process.

ADDICTIONS AND THE SPIRITUAL LIFE

All addictions have spiritual roots. Human nature is inherently rebellious and selfish. It desires self-aggrandizement and self-satisfaction. Addictions are a direct reflection and outcome of our life of bondage to this rebellion— traditionally called sin. No healing is complete, as I have repeatedly said in this book, that does not address and remove this bondage.

But addictions not only have spiritual *causes*; they have spiritual *consequences*. There are many ways in which addictions can be spiritually destructive:

- *They are forms of spiritual idolatry.* One worships the thing or behavior that is addicting.
- *They sap energy and demand attention,* so that one is distracted from spiritual activity.
- *They erode spiritual gains* by causing a constant feeling of failure.
- *They create a false barrier between the addict and God,* a barrier of guilt that will not and cannot receive forgiveness because forgiveness requires repentance and a giving up of the addiction.
- *They prevent obedience to God* because addiction keeps the victim focused on the "flesh" and its need for pleasure.
- *They perpetuate sin,* and sin is displeasing to God.

Because addictions involve the spirit, healing must involve the spirit as well. And spiritual healing begins with *repentance*—whether the addiction is to narcotics, food, money, gambling, jogging, codependency, sex, or religion. Addictions are also temptations—temptations to engage in sinful behavior.

To bring your addiction under control, then, you have to say, with Jesus, "Get thee behind me, Satan." You have to affirm the truth that "Thou shalt worship the Lord thy God, and him only shalt thou serve" (Mt 4:10). Then, and then only, will the prison gates open to let you out of your addiction.

Addiction is enslavement. You sell your body, mind, and spirit to an idea, a compulsion, or a craving. In this sense, then, addiction controls us. As such, it is sin, even if it does no harm to another living soul. To match up particular addictions with specific sins, of course, would be simplistic and ridiculous. But addictions *in general* are a consequence of the Fall. If we were not sinful by nature, our only compulsions would be *positive* ones—seeking to glorify God in all we do and say. So we cannot escape the relationship between addiction and evil, between our compulsions and our rebellion.

The way out of the addiction *begins*, therefore, with an acknowledgment of our sinfulness and a decision to turn aside from the temptation the addiction offers. "Get thee behind me, Satan" needs to be our constant prayer. This is repentance.

But repentance is *only the beginning*. Just as an addiction cannot be defeated by willpower alone, neither can it be overcome by dumping the whole problem in God's lap. There are those who believe turning to God with a problem means you simply hand over the reins of the problem to him and then go sit in the back of the wagon. You don't have to change or work up any sweat; God does it all for you. Next thing you know, God has worked his miracle, and you are all recovered.

That's *not* how it works. I agree entirely with Dr. Gerald May who says, *"The power of grace flows most fully when human*

will chooses to act in harmony with divine will."[1]
Did you get that? Read it again! I think it is crucial.

What this means is that God *expects* us to cooperate with
him in our sanctification. He *demands* that we own up to our
problems and participate in his work of grace, accepting
responsibility for our sinful contribution and then acting in
obedience to his commands.

In working with parents and kids over the years, I have
frequently known mothers or fathers who do their children's homework for them. Can you believe it? Here is a kid
who has been given a homework assignment *for his good*. The
teacher believes that working the math problems or writing
an essay at home after school helps the kid to learn! But what
do these parents do? They complete the work themselves
while Johnny watches TV for several hours or Mary visits
with her friends.

When I challenge these parents, their response is usually
something like, "But he will fail in class." Or, "Mary has so
few friends. I think it's important that she visit with the ones
she does have." They miss the point. Homework is part of
the learning process. Parents who intercept homework
hinder learning.

But this is precisely what we often expect God to do for us!
"Lord," we in effect pray, "You know what a tough time I've
had today. I really would appreciate it if you would just
work a miracle and get this problem off my back. I know I
should go and apologize and own up to my selfishness, but
it would be so much more convenient for me if you would
just work it all out." We treat God as if he were an indulgent
parent who feels guilty for making us work so hard—or who
didn't quite make it in his own life and therefore needs to
fulfill himself through our succeeding! This is the essence of
immaturity.

What God expects and demands in the process of
overcoming addiction is that we stay right there in the

struggle, confronting our dishonesty, denial, or defenses and remaining fully aware of the learning that must take place. He provides the awareness; we must make the decisions. He points out the weakness; we must claim the power to overcome the weakness. He shows us where we have failed; we must go and put things right. We cannot short-circuit God's homework.

It is true that at times God does rescue us without much help (or interference) on our part. Why he sometimes does this, even before we have learned whatever lesson there is to learn, only he knows. But in all his work in our lives, this theme is clear: He is always more interested in our sanctification and growth than he is in making life simple and easy for us. We want to avoid growing pains; he sees the potential for our achieving maturity through pain. If we are wise, we will take his way.

First Corinthians 10:13 was one of the very first verses of Scripture I memorized after becoming a Christian at age seventeen, and it has been precious and comforting to me ever since. This profound verse reminds us of several important truths that can help us respond to temptation and continue to grow:

1. *We are all in the same boat.* Wrong desires are neither new nor different. Many before us have faced exactly the same temptations.

2. *We can trust God to keep temptation within boundaries* so that we can stand up against it.

3. *He will "make a way to escape."* This is the truth that has always impressed me the most. In other words, *God doesn't remove us from the temptations; he shows us the way out.* Then it is up to us to walk the way he shows us! We are left with the responsibility to exercise our free will, surrender our personal desires, and in humility and with dignity leave the temptation behind.

When we do this, the real miracle happens. The moment

we take the first step of obedience, God turns on the "after burners" (the parts that give jet engines extra thrust). His power then continues to sustain us in our obedience.

POSITIVE ADDICTIONS?

After coming down so hard on all addictions, it may seem a little strange that I should hint that there may be "positive" addictions as well. Actually, since destructiveness is one of the identifying characteristics of addictions, the term wouldn't really apply. But there are ingrained habits, powerful cravings, and strong attachments that are clearly positive in their effect. Some people label these "positive addictions."

When you examine human behavior, you don't have to look far to find these healthy attachments and desires. We must crave food in general, for instance, or else we would not survive. And as I pointed out in an earlier chapter, at certain times in our lives we may develop particular cravings for nutrients our bodies need. The obvious example for this is the strange cravings many pregnant women develop—peanut butter on pickles, ketchup on tomatoes, aerosol cheese on fudge. These cravings usually come on in the middle of the night, and they're usually obtainable only by a midnight trip to a twenty-four hour supermarket! But I believe these cravings must have a basis in real physical need.

One can hardly say that a basic and persistent need like this is part of an addiction. Clearly it is positive, because the final consequence is positive.

Here's another example. Suppose that a friend has just had a major setback in her life. Her fiancé, whom she deeply loves, has decided to abandon the relationship. She is devastated and needs someone to talk to. Now, you are not feeling so great yourself. You've got problems at work, your son has broken an arm, and your husband is away on an extended business trip. The natural impulse would be to tell your friend to "get lost," "grow up," or "go see a shrink"— you're too busy to help. But you have been working in your personal life on developing the *habit of love*. And out of that habit, your first response is love and concern. You listen and you help, putting your own needs on hold.

Now this kind of instinctive love and concern is a *positive habit*. It may not feel good at the time you do it, but it will feel good afterward. And you know that the more you practice this habit the more you will be shaped by it.

G. Alan Marlatt, a prominent researcher in the field of addictions, does believes that "positive lifestyle activities can themselves become *addictive* as they develop into regular habits."[2] He defines a *negative addiction* as an activity that feels good in the short run but has negative effects in the long run. A *positive addiction*, on the other hand, is a habit that often feels unpleasant in the short run but is ultimately associated with positive consequences. For instance, someone starting an exercise program may feel a lot of pain at first, but later will begin to reap the benefits of the exercise— increased flexibility, heightened energy, and an enhanced feeling of well-being following a vigorous physical workout.

Positive attachments are possible, therefore, whether or not we call them addictions. Actually, they may not be more than "habits" in the sense that one is not compelled to perform them but chooses to, and there is no loss of control. William Glasser, the proponent of *Reality Therapy*, identifies six criteria that must be met for such a habitual activity to be positive:[3]

- It should be *noncompetitive*.
- You should be able to do it easily and without extraordinary effort.

- You should be able to do it alone or rarely with others.
- You should believe it has some value (physical, mental, or spiritual) *for you.*
- You should be the only one who decides whether or not you are getting better at it.
- The activity *must* be such that you can do it *without criticizing yourself.*

The element of doing the activity alone is crucial. Any time you introduce someone else into the picture, you introduce *competition, criticism,* or both. At that moment, the attachment becomes negative and could become a negative addiction, even though it is exactly the same activity.

Running is a good example here. As long as it is non-competitive, done without extraordinary effort or damaging consequences, it has great value for you, and doesn't create self-criticism. Clearly it is a positive attachment. But let us suppose you run with a friend. You both have a competitive spirit. You want to be a better, faster, more enduring (or whatever) runner than her. If she's better than you, you begin to resent it. You begin to criticize her and yourself mentally while you run. You are driven to outdo her. Now your running is no longer a positive addiction. It has turned sour, and it may well become an addiction.

I would add one further criterion for a positive attachment to the list cited above: The activity should not be a way of covering up or avoiding feelings.

Take the running example again. If you go out and run whenever you get upset, and if your running becomes a way of avoiding feelings or a spouse that you are mad at, or removes you from pain you haven't confronted, then your running begins to look like an addiction. You are using it just as an alcoholic uses alcohol—to anesthetize the reality of life.

These distinctions also help us to look at the difference between "workaholism" and plain old hard work. True workaholics are always "playing to an audience." This competitive element can be in the past (proving to a dead father that you amount to something), the present (proving you are better than the person next to you), or the future (building more security than anyone else). Workaholics are also extremely self-critical; often their major motivating gimmick is to flog themselves into greater achievements. But above all, the true workaholic uses the work as a form of escape to avoid the real issues of life.

POSITIVE SPIRITUAL ATTACHMENTS

If there are *positive spiritual attachments* (or just plain "good habits" if you want to call them that), what are they? Allow me to suggest a few. You may wish to reflect on these and consider whether any or all of them are worthy of developing:

Reading Scripture. This can be done both for encouragement and for spiritual enhancement. While it is possible to turn the Bible into a fetish, most of us don't suffer from this problem. Our problem is usually quite the reverse; we don't give ourselves to Scripture with enough intensity. I believe that Scripture, in the hands of the Holy Spirit, is a powerful therapeutic resource, useful in healing both our spirits and our psyches. This is what Scripture has to say about itself:

For whatever God says to us is full of living power: it is sharper than the sharpest dagger, cutting swift and deep into our innermost thoughts and desires with all their parts, exposing us for what we really are. Heb 4:12 LB

They didn't have scalpels in New Testament times. If they had, I think *scalpel* would have replaced the word *dagger*. God's Word is a scalpel in the hands of a skilled Surgeon who knows where the emotional or spiritual cancer is and can go straight to the source of pain and sickness. Let us aspire, then, to be truly "hooked" on God's Word. It can only bring healing, never destruction.

Prayer. Of all the spiritual disciplines, prayer seems to be the hardest to develop. At least that's what I've seen in my many years of counseling Christians. Clearly it is a habit that must be deliberately cultivated in the midst of our hurly-burly, hurried lifestyles. Don't be embarrassed to admit that you struggle in this area. God knows all about it anyway.

One reason I believe prayer is so difficult for us is that private prayer is usually carried out silently. Silent praying, as with silent reading, is a modern phenomenon—the by-product of living close together in urban settings. In New Testament times, praying and reading was always done out loud. In fact, Jesus' admonition to his followers to go into a closet (off by ourselves) to pray was *not* an admonition to pray silently; it was a criticism of the hypocrites who prayed standing in public places (Mt 6:5). We need a "closet" for prayers because our prayers make noise—or at least they ought to. Speaking your prayers out loud can be a refreshing and meaningful experience. You'll have to find a private place to do it, but I commend it as a helpful encouragement.

There are many books available to help you in your prayer life, so I won't attempt an exhaustive summary of help here. I will simply make a few suggestions for how you can improve your prayer life:

1. *Simplify your praying as much as possible.* Prayer takes many forms—contemplative, thanksgiving, requesting. It should also include waiting quietly so that you can be instructed by God.

2. *The attitude of prayer should always be the same:* a simple waiting upon God and an experiencing of his presence in humility.

3. *You should develop the prayer of "being" in addition to the*

prayer of "asking." The prayer of "being" is the prayer that only asks to experience God's presence. Such a prayer is *receptive* rather than *expressive.* It does not command God. It asks for no benefit. It appreciates God for who he is, not for what he can give. This kind of prayer is a habit we neglect to our detriment. We are the losers for not being in communion with God.

Solitude. Most of us are strongly attached (some to the point of addiction) to activity and people. We don't like being alone or having nothing to do. Our adrenaline level drops uncomfortably low when there is silence and no stimulation. So we reach for the radio or TV and bring the world to us if we cannot be with it.

But there can be no spiritual vitality without some degree of *solitude.* Our cravings for stimulation, crowds, noise, entertainment, activity, and achieving must at times be set aside so that we can seek God in stillness. We must let the adrenaline that is surging through our arteries and vital organs subside and tune in to the "still, small voice" of God. In this we have the example of Jesus who, when he wanted to commune with the Father, turned away from the needy crowd and sought out a garden or a hillside. We must learn to be comfortable with solitude or being alone so that we can turn from our restlessness, drivenness, and compulsiveness and find peace.

Once you have tasted of this solitude you can very well become hooked on it—in a positive sense, of course. It is in solitude that you can learn to face yourself courageously, not concerned whether you are making the right impression or saying the right thing. You can just be yourself in simplicity and without complication. Perhaps you don't really know yourself. If so, this is the way to get acquainted.

Solitude is also the place where you can examine yourself and "see if there be any wicked way" in you (Ps 139:24). *The unexamined life is not worth living.* I think it was Socrates who originally said this. The self who never takes a good look in the mirror of honesty will never really grow.

Now, I realize that I have not spelled out the *how* of solitude. It is impossible to do this in a general way because lives differ so greatly. Some may have the benefit of working in a quiet, still place and can find their time of solitude without difficulty. Some may need to be courageous and shut their office door for a while each day and hang a "Do Not Disturb" sign on the handle. Others may need to get up earlier and take a long walk or go sit in the park to find a quiet place. A mother with a newborn baby may be able to use the hours of feeding for her quiet time. The problem is not the *how* but the *when*. Unless you give priority to your times of solitude, they will never happen.

This leads me to my concluding thought for this book. It has to do with *time*. Whether we are actually struggling to overcome an addiction problem or trying to develop the spiritual strength never to develop one, the problem is always time—we can never get enough of it!

On the one hand, we make an idol of it. We use it to the max. We save time by doing more than one thing at any moment. When we're stuck in traffic, we try to catch up on the news. When we dry our hair, we try to make up a list of things to do. (If you are like me, you always take something to read when in the bathroom.) "Time is money" is the motto of our world. Time is our most valued commodity. Queen Elizabeth I cried out in her dying moments, "All my possessions for a moment of time." And that was in 1603—long before alarm clocks, traffic jams, or fast food! We know how she felt!

But when it comes to changing some habit or working on a personal problem, what is our most common excuse? "I don't have any time!" To spend time in Christian meditation or reflection on God's Word takes time. Historian Will Durant once said, "No person who is in a hurry is quite civilized." Similarly, no one who is in a hurry is growing spiritually. The pace of change and a work ethic that has "gone mad" is robbing us of an essential ingredient in spiritual development: time to reflect, to examine ourselves, to be receptive to the promptings of God.

Listen to a prayer of Moses, that great man of God. As we close this book make it your prayer also:

Seventy years are given us! And some may even live to eighty. But even the best of these years are often emptiness and pain; soon they disappear, and we are gone. . . . Teach us to number our days and recognize how few they are; help us to spend them as we should.

Ps 90:10, 12 LB

Referral Resources

THE FOLLOWING ARE NAMES AND ADDRESSES of organizations that may be helpful to you when you are searching for professional help. Although all but one of these organizations are based in California, they can refer you to counselors across the country:

Fuller Theological Seminary
Graduate School of Psychology
180 N. Oakland Ave.
Pasadena, CA 91101
(818) 584-5507

Focus on the Family
801 Corporate Center Dr.
Pomona, CA 91799

Rosemead School of Psychology
13800 Biola Ave.
La Mirada, CA 90639
(213) 903-4867

The Christian Association for Psychological Studies
Dr. J. Harold Ellens
26705 Farmington Road
Farmington Hills, MI 48018
(313) 447-1350
or

Dr. Robert R. King
P.O. Box 789
Blue Jay, CA 92317
(714) 337-0838

The following is a list of twelve-step programs which you may find in your local telephone directory:

AA—Alcoholics Anonymous
Al-Anon—Family and Friends of Alcoholics
ACOA—Adult Children of Alcoholics
CA—Cocaine Anonymous
EHA—Emotional Health Anonymous
FA—Families Anonymous (Family and friends of drug users)
GA—Gamblers Anonymous
ISA—Incest Survivors Anonymous
NA—Narcotics Anonymous
Nar-Anon—Family and Friends of Substance Abusers
OA—Overeaters Anonymous
PA—Parents Anonymous, for parents who may endanger their children
SAA—Sex Addicts Anonymous
Spender Menders—for those with a spending addiction

Other programs that may be helpful:

ACT—Addiction Counseling Treatment
Parent Alert
Toughlove—for families of substance abusers

The following organizations with addresses may help you to get in touch with a local chapter:

Sex Addicts Anonymous
Twin Cities S.A.A.
P.O. Box 3038
Minneapolis, MN 53403
(213) 386-8789

Overeaters Anonymous
P.O. Box 92870
Los Angeles, CA 90009
(213) 320-7941

Gamblers Anonymous
National Service Office
P.O. Box 17173
Los Angeles, CA 90017

Narcotics Anonymous
World Service Office
16155 Wyandott St.
Van Nuys, CA 91406
(818) 780-3951

Spender Menders
P.O. Box 15000-156
San Francisco, CA 94115
(415) 773-9754

Notes

Introduction
The Addiction Controversy

1. Gerald G. May, *Addiction and Grace* (San Francisco: Harper & Row, 1988), 3.
2. Ibid., 4.

ONE
What Are Hidden Addictions?

1. American Psychiatric Association, *Diagnostic and Statistical Manual of Mental Disorders DSM-III-R*, 3d ed. rev. (Washington, D.C.: American Psychiatric Association, 1987).
2. Webster's New Twentieth Century Dictionary (unabridged), second edition (New York: World Publishing Co., 1975).
3. Lawrence J. Hatterer, *The Pleasure Addicts* (New York: A.S. Barnes & Co., 1980), 17.
4. Timothy B. Baker, "Special Issue: Models of Addiction," Journal of Abnormal Psychology, (May 1988), 117.
5. Ibid.
6. J. Keith Miller, *Sin: Overcoming the Ultimate Deadly Addiction* (San Francisco: Harper & Row, 1987), 45.

TWO
Addictions and Cravings

1. Roy A. Wise, "The Neurobiology of Craving: Implications for the Understanding and Treatment of Addiction," *Journal of Abnormal Psychology*, (Vol. 97, No. 2, 1988), 18.
2. Ibid., 118.
3. Ibid., 125.

THREE
Is There an Addictive Personality?

1. M.M. Glatt and J. Marks, *The Dependence Phenomenon* (New Jersey: George A. Bodgen and Sons, 1982), 14.
2. Henry E. Adams and Patricia B. Sutker, eds., *Handbook of Psychopathology* (New York: Plenum Press, 1984), 626.

SIX
Lifestyle Addictions

1. Anthony Campolo, *Seven Deadly Sins* (Wheaton, IL: Victor Books, 1987), 142-43.
2. *Newsweek,* December 4, 1989, 17.
3. Frank B. Minirth et al, *The Workaholic and His Family: An Inside Look* (Grand Rapids: Baker Books, 1981).
4. Judith K. Sprankle and Henry Ebel, *The Workaholic Syndrome* (New York: Walker & Co., 1982).

SEVEN
Codependency (Addiction to Helping)

1. Melody Beattie, *Codependent No More* (New York: Harper/ Hazelden, 1987), 6.
2. Ibid., 45.
3. Ibid., 11.
4. Jim and Phyllis Alsdurf, "The Generic Disease," *Christianity Today* (Dec. 9, 1988), 30-38.
5. Edwin H. Friedman, *Generation to Generation* (New York: The Guilford Press, 1985), 45.
6. Anne Wilson Schaef, *Co-dependence: Misunderstood and Mistreated* (San Francisco: Harper & Row, 1986), 41.

EIGHT
Religious Addiction

1. Teresa of Avila, *Interior Castle,* quoted in Benedict J.Groeschel, *Spiritual Passages* (New York: Crossroad Publishing Co., 1986), 182.
2 W. Allport Gordon, *The Individual and His Religion* (New York: The MacMillan Company, 1950), 113.

NINE
Addictions to Sex and Love

1. Jerrold S. Greenberg, Clint E. Bruess, and Doris W. Sands,

Sexuality: Insights and Issues (Dubuque, Iowa: Wm. C. Brown, 1986), 139.
2. Ibid., 292.
3. Archibald D. Hart, *Unlocking the Mystery of Your Emotions* (Dallas, Texas: WORD Publishing, 1989), Chapter 8.
4. Ibid.
5. "Great Sex: Reclaiming a Christian Sexual Ethic," *Christianity Today* (October 1, 1987), 33.
6. From *What I Believe,* quoted by an anonymous pastor in "The War Within," *Sins of the Body*, Terry C. Muck, ed., (Dallas, Texas: WORD Publishing, 1989), 37.
7. Ibid., 21.
8. *Psychology Today,* December 1989, 80.
9. "Great Sex," *Christianity Today*, 33.

TEN
Addiction to Adrenaline

1. Archibald D. Hart, *The Hidden Link Between Adrenaline and Stress* (Dallas, Texas: WORD Publishing, 1986), 67-82.
2. Harvey B. Milkman and Stanley G. Sunderwirth, *Craving for Ecstasy,* (Lexington, Massachusetts: Lexington Books, 1987), xiv.
3. Ibid., 6.
4. See my book *Overcoming Anxiety* for a discussion of panic anxiety.
5. See my book *The Hidden Link Between Adrenaline and Stress* for a more complete treatment of these skills.
6. Frank B. Gilbreth and Ernestine G. Carey, *Cheaper by the Dozen* (New York: T.Y. Crowell Co., 1963).
7. Brother Lawrence of the Resurrection, *The Practice of the Presence of God* translated by John J. Delaney (Garden City, New York: Image Books, 1977).

ELEVEN
Addictions to Food

1. David G. Benner, *Baker Encyclopedia of Psychology* (Grand Rapids, Michigan: Baker Book House, 1985), 767.

TWELVE
Overcoming Your Hidden Addiction

1. Ernest Becker, *The Denial of Death* (New York: The Free Press, 1973).

2. Ibid., 204.
3. Ibid., 270.
4. Ibid., 271.
5. Ibid., 271.
6. Archibald D. Hart, *The Hidden Link Between Adrenaline and Stress* (Dallas, Texas: WORD Publishing, 1986), Chapter 12.
7. Ibid., chapter 11.
8. Ibid., chapter 10.
9. *Pastoral Renewal* (Ann Arbor, Michigan: Servant Ministries— The Center for Pastoral Renewal).
10. "Report on the Institute for Christian Living," *Christianity Today* (December 9, 1988): 31.

THIRTEEN
A Theology for Self-Control

1. Gerald G. May, *Addiction and Grace*, (San Francisco, CA: Harper and Row, 1988), 139.
2. G. Alan Marlatt and Judith R. Gordon, *Relapse Prevention* (New York: The Guilford Press, 1985), 299.
3. Ibid, 299.

Another Book of Interest from Servant Publications

Making Choices
Practical Wisdom for Everyday Moral Decisions
Peter Kreeft

"It's a moral jungle out there," writes Peter Kreeft. In *Making Choices*, he describes why we find decision-making so difficult and living with our choices even harder. With penetrating wisdom, good humor, and common sense, Peter Kreeft draws a map through the everyday jungle of moral choices, one simple enough for the believer and convincing enough for the skeptic. *$8.95*